COLLEGE
WRITING

COLLEGE WRITING

A Personal Approach to Academic Writing

Toby Fulwiler
University of Vermont

BOYNTON/COOK PUBLISHERS
HEINEMANN
Portsmouth, NH

BOYNTON/COOK PUBLISHERS, INC.
A Subsidiary of
HEINEMANN EDUCATIONAL BOOKS, INC.
361 Hanover Street, Portsmouth, NH 03801-3959

Previous edition first published by Scott, Foresman and Company under the title *College Writing*.

The following have generously given permission to use quotations from copyrighted work:

Page 14: "Buffalo Bill's" is reprinted from *Tulips & Chimneys* by E.E. Cummings, edited by George James Firmage, by permission of Liveright Publishing Corporation. Copyright 1923, 1925, and renewed 1951, 1953 by E.E. Cummings. Copyright © 1973, 1976 by the Trustees for the E.E. Cummings Trust. Copyright © 1973, 1976 by George James Firmage.

Pages 63–64: Excerpts from "Living Like Weasles" from *TEACHING A STONE TO TALK: Expeditions and Encounters* by Annie Dillard. Copyright © 1982 by Annie Dillard. Reprinted by permission of HarperCollins Publishers Inc.

Every effort has been made to contact the copyright holders for permission to reprint borrowed material. We regret any oversights that may have occurred and would be happy to rectify them in future printings of this work.

Library of Congress Cataloging-in-Publication Data
Fulwiler, Toby, 1942–
    College writing : a personal approach to academic writing / Toby
Fulwiler.
        p.   cm.
    Includes index.
    ISBN 0-86709-290-4
    1. English language—Rhetoric.   I. Title.
PE1408F8 191
808'.042—dc20   91-20380
                                                                      CIP

Cover design by Jenny Greenleaf
Printed in the United States of America
92 93 94 95   10 9 8 7 6 5 4 3 2

Contents

Preface   *vii*
Acknowledgments   *ix*

Part I   WRITING TO LEARN   1

  1   Writing in the Academic Community   *3*
  2   Thinking with Writing   *11*
  3   Writing to Solve Problems   *20*
  4   The Writer's Journal   *32*
  5   Journal Writing: How To   *43*

Part II   WRITING FOR READERS   51

  6   The Role of Audiences   *53*
  7   Writing from Experience   *62*
  8   Writing Expository Essays   *78*
  9   Writing Interpretive Essays   *90*
  10   Set Pieces   *101*
  11   Imaginative Writing   *112*
  12   Composing: How To   *123*

Part III   WRITING AND RESEARCH   133

  13   Finding Research Questions   *135*
  14   The Research Log   *142*
  15   Resources: People and Places   *151*

16 Resources: Books and Periodicals *160*
17 The Use of Authority *166*
18 Finding Your Voice *177*

Postscript One: Writing with Computers *189*
Postscript Two: Guidelines for Writing
  Groups *194*
Postscript Three: Advice to Poor Spellers *199*
Postscript Four: A Short Guide to
  Punctuation *202*
Index *209*

Preface

I have written *College Writing* in the belief that learning to write well in college is not all that mysterious. College writers need to understand how their academic community works and why. They need to learn a few forms, conventions, and guidelines. And they need to practice writing for a variety of purposes to different audiences.

College Writing provides brief discussions of specific college writing assignments, including formal and informal essays, examinations, reports, and journals. In addition, it describes general strategies for revision, editing, research, and problem solving. I believe that certain kinds of students will find this book especially useful:

1. Students who enjoy writing, who already write well, but could always use a few more strategies.
2. Those who have never before enjoyed writing, but for whom this book may come as a pleasant surprise.
3. Those planning to major in the liberal arts, who would enjoy an introduction to the variety of writing possible in a college community.
4. Those *not* majoring in the liberal arts, who will find in this book a useful guide for writing well in any field of study.

I also believe that certain kinds of writing instructors will find this book especially useful:

1. Instructors who enjoy teaching writing and do it well, but might like their students to read a series of short essays on writing in a college setting.

2. Those who plan to spend most classroom time with their students' own writing; who believe that writers gain most by reading and commenting on each other's writing.

3. Those who believe writing to learn is as important as learning to write and that both can be pleasant and provocative activities.

4. Those who view research as a lively investigative activity; who believe that researching means learning to observe and interview as well as visit card catalogues and compile bibliographies.

In other words, *College Writing* is written to students and instructors who believe that writing is central to the whole academic enterprise, that it is at once a tough and wonderful business, and that it can be both learned and taught. It is also written to students and instructors who do not believe these things but think they might be worth considering.

Toby Fulwiler

Acknowledgments

Thanks to Bob Boynton and all the Heinemann folks for continuing to be the best publisher around. Thanks, especially, to Peter Stillman for being the best editor, critic, and gadfly, for incessantly asking about the exercises in this book: "Would I want to do that?" Thanks, also, to the many students in Wisconsin, Michigan, and Vermont who taught me to teach writing. And thanks to Anna, Megan, and Laura for giving me time to write and stories to write with.

Toby Fulwiler

Part I

WRITING TO LEARN

Chapter 1

WRITING IN THE ACADEMIC COMMUNITY

Professional writers write most confidently when they understand their subject, know their purpose, and can successfully predict their readers' response. The same holds for student writers, of course. But to become adept at college writing you will need to understand, above all, the nature and purpose of the academic community in which you write and the nature and expectations of your academic audience. Each new course you take will teach you a little more about this community in which you now dwell. This book is written to introduce you to some of the general expectations and practices typical of college communities—essential knowledge for writing successfully in college. If you learn your way around generally at first, you will be well prepared to move around more specifically later on, as you major in and master particular areas of study.

Knowing your way around the academic community will simplify and clarify your writing tasks, but in no way will *guarantee* speedy and successful results. In fact, there are no guarantees for any writers—even those with experience. Each time you put pen to paper or fingers to keyboard, the whole mystifying process of composing begins anew. If you are an experienced writer, you already know this and accept the difficulty and unpredictability as part of the process.

If you have not had much writing experience, you may believe that everyone else finds writing easier than you do. This is seldom so. Writing—especially academic writing—is difficult for even the most experienced writers; but they may have more confidence that, in the end, it will turn out all right, more knowledge of the tasks before them, and probably more strategies to help them accomplish those tasks.

PURPOSE

To write well, you need to know *why* you are writing in the first place. What is it you want to say about what? Sometimes that has been decided for you, as when a teacher makes a specific writing assignment or when an editor commissions a particular piece for a magazine. At other times the act of writing might be your idea completely, as when you decide to do an extra credit project or to keep a personal journal. However, regardless of the initial motivation behind a piece of writing, once committed to it, you must do two things: figure out your own particular approach to the subject, and write from knowledge about it—which may mean searching carefully through your memory, reading more, or simply constructing an argument in the most logical way possible.

I take as a given that you can't write well about something you don't understand. You can, of course, raise good questions and pose problems related to what is new or confusing to you, but beyond that there is little you can compose except BS—and we all know the value of that. The first part of this book explains how writing can actually lead you to more complete knowledge about something, which will enable you later to write to someone else with some authority. Most meaningful knowledge in a school setting is gained through some exploration in language and is subsequently expressed in writing.

To create an effective piece of writing you should know about accepted ways of thinking about your subject and conventional forms of handling and expressing your knowledge of it. What you particularly need to know are the expectations and assumptions of the community in which your assignment is taking place.

THE ACADEMIC COMMUNITY

If you are reading this book while enrolled in college, you are already a member of an academic community. What, you may ask, is the big deal? I'm in school, I'm studying, taking tests, writing papers, and getting grades—as I've done since first grade. What's the difference? Well, this time there may be a difference that could influence everything you write. Let's look at the nature of a college academic community.

College and university communities were established to study something called the truth. Each discipline pursues, investigates, and teaches some small part of it: the sciences investigate what is true in the natural world, the social sciences the social world, the humanities the individual world, the arts the aesthetic world, and so on. Of course, truth is seldom packaged in tight disciplinary units, so understanding something fully often requires the crossing of disciplinary lines. The most extreme case may be the study of literature, in which to understand what is true about a single novel by Charles Dickens or Virginia Woolf you may need to know some history, philosophy, psychology, physics, anthropology, economics, or politics. In some cases, new hybrid disciplines have been created at the juncture where one pursuit of truth meets another—for example, biochemistry, psycholinguistics, and social anthropology.

To establish truth about the physical world, scientists have developed a particular way of asking questions and looking for answers which is called "the scientific method." Finding out biological or chemical truth may require similar methods but different tools. Those who investigate the social world—sociologists, economists, political scientists, psychologists, geographers, and anthropologists—have, in many instances, adopted the scientist's methodologies. They often find, of course, that the social world is even harder to pin down for examination than even the most distant star or complex microorganism.

To establish truth in the so-called humanistic world, humanists—philosophers, literary scholars, and historians—have developed a potpourri of investigative methods, ranging from the scientific to the imaginative and intuitive. In contrast, practitioners of the arts—musicians, composers, poets, novelists, playwrights, directors, actors, painters, sculptors, and dancers—do their best to escape classification of any kind. Neat disciplinary categories become increasingly messy when you realize that historians study social behavior but are usually called humanists, and that psychologists, who study individual behavior, are usually called social scientists, as are the geographers who study the physical space of the earth.

Furthermore, the professional schools of business, law, education, agriculture, health, natural resources, and engineering have put together their own specialized programs to train people to do certain highly specialized work in the larger community. As part of the process of training, these schools require at least an introductory-level knowledge of the different disciplines.

Despite these differences, many fields of study make assumptions about teaching, learning, and knowledge that have more in common than not—which is why we can even talk about the academic community as an entity. In fact, if you look at the modes of establishing truth in disciplines as different as history and physics, you may be more surprised by the assumptions on which they agree than those on which they differ. For example, both historians and physicists depend heavily on close observation for the accumulation of facts on which to make generalizations, which they then try to disprove. Biologists and English teachers, too, may have more in common than meets the casual eye.

THE GROUND RULES

Certain beliefs operate as glue to hold together the otherwise disparate community of teachers and students that compose the academic community: you cannot write successful college-level papers without understanding these things.

Belief

As both student and writer, it helps to remember that establishing belief is the job of (1) the entire university community, (2) each general field of study within the university, and (3) each individual student writer in each particular course in that community. There is a necessary relationship among these three elements which is relevant to every single act of communication or expression you do while a member of this community. You want those who read your laboratory reports, term papers, and essay tests to believe that what you say is essentially *true*. Your job as a college writer is to persuade your readers that what you say is true, which introduces another element.

Persuasion

Every serious act of writing is essentially an exercise in persuasion: if you describe an experiment, you want your description to *persuade* your chemistry teacher that this is what actually happened; if you analyze the major causes of the Civil War, you want to convince your history teacher that, yes, these were the causes; if you evaluate the merits of a Robert Frost poem, you want your English teacher to believe your evaluation. While this may seem obvious, you must remember that persuasion is also the goal of most advertisements and political propaganda, but something rather important sets persuasion in the academic world apart from persuasion in the world of profit and politics: the use of evidence.

Evidence

How writers create belief is largely a matter of how they marshal their *evidence* to support what they say. In the first place, there must *be* evidence to back up any assertions; otherwise, they are unsupported or weak generalizations. In the academic world, there is often a premium on evidence derived from books—preferably numerous books, each written by an expert with credentials that can be checked. Depending on your discipline, of course, other sources of evidence might be observation, experimentation, statistics, interviews, or personal experience—each documented in some verifiable way.

Documentation

To make an assertion as convincing as possible in the academic community, you should always provide your audience with a complete account of where you got your information, ideas, or evidence (more on this in Chapters 13–17); hence, the importance of footnotes, endnotes, references, bibliographies, and literature searches. Essentially, your readers want to know *who* said *what*, *where*, and *when*. When you provide this information, readers believe that your student ideas are buttressed by expert ideas and are more likely to believe them. In college writing you ignore documentation at your peril.

Subjectivity

In many disciplines, your personal opinion may not be worth very much; in some it will be. In the more interpretive disciplines, such as history, philosophy, and literature, you will generally find more room for *personal interpretation* than in the more quantitative disciplines, such as chemistry, physics, and mathematics. (The social sciences fall somewhere in between.) To be safe, whenever you make an academic assertion in any discipline, use the best evidence you can find and document it. But in all disciplines, your own reasoned, and necessarily subjective, judgment will at some times be necessary; if it is, just be sure to state it as such ("In my opinion. . . ." or, "It seems to me. . . .") and give the best reasons you can.

Objectivity

In the academic community, the way in which you search for truth is supposed to be *impartial* and *objective*, with some very clear exceptions within the humanities and fine arts. For many disciplines, however, when you perform experiments and do research, you attempt to remove yourself from the situation as much as possible and attempt to demonstrate that the results of your work are objectively, not subjectively, true; that is, that the results you are reporting are not a figment of your imagination and personal bias and that anybody else doing this work would find the same results. In science, the best experiments are replicable (repeatable) by other scientists; the social sciences generally try to follow suit. This point is important to you as a writer because it means that it's advisable, whenever possible, to mention how you got your results (by objective methods, of course). In some cases, it's even preferable to use a deliberately objective tone (passive constructions, no first-person pronouns) and quantitative detail (statistics, graphs) in your writing, if you want to persuade members of these more or less objective communities to believe you.

Relativity

Students of even the most objective scientific disciplines make absolute statements at their peril. In the twentieth century, especially since Einstein, *relativity* has been the watchword: there is no such thing as certainty in the physical universe, and that concept has filtered, in one way or another, into every field of study. We now believe that there is more than one possible explanation, more than one possible interpretation, more than one version of nearly everything that happens. How does this apply to your writing? Quite simply, every statement you make within the academic community will be subject to question, objection, interpretation, and cross-examination; the farther you progress in your studies, the more likely it is that your ideas will be challenged. As a result, when you make academic assertions, pay attention to the qualifying words (perhaps, maybe, possibly, actually) and tentative phrases ("Have you considered. . . ?" "It is likely. . . ." "In my judgment. . . ." and "In all probability. . . ."). These phrases signify that you recognize the tentative nature of the "truth." So, though you *try* to be objective in your work or writing, you also need to acknowledge that it is ultimately impossible.

Balance

My last observation about the academic community is related to the notions of objectivity and relativity. Because there are multiple interpretations for so much that happens in the natural and social worlds—multiple versions of right and wrong, good and bad, correct and incorrect—it becomes useful for writers to represent these possibilities in their discourse through assertions that give *fair* (honest, nonemotional) treatment even to positions with which the writer disagrees. Important here are balance phrases ("On one hand/on the other hand. . . ." "However, . . .") and the recognition of multiple causes ("in the first place/in the second place," "in addition," "also," "finally"). When you use these phrases in your spoken and written language, they suggest that you know the rules of the academic community.

Unfortunately, the foregoing generalizations are just that, generalizations that we don't have time to explore fully. In fact, the only thorough elaboration takes place semester by semester as you are progressively initiated into membership in the world of college or university studies. But no discussion of writing formal academic papers is useful unless you understand generally the nature and context of your academic audience. Every suggestion in this book is predicated on your understanding of this community and its ground rules and expectations. Once understood and agreed to, the many seemingly arbitrary assignments you will receive may begin to make better sense to you, and, in turn, your handling of them as a writer will make better sense to your teachers.

HOW THIS BOOK WORKS

This book examines three roles that writing plays in the academic community: a mode of thought, a mode of communication, and a mode of research. Chapters 1 through 5 explore the role of writing as a tool for developing your critical thinking skills. Chapters 6 through 12 describe the forms of writing in which students (and faculty) most often report their thoughts. Chapters 13 through 17 examine the role of research in substantiating these thoughts. Finally, Chapter 18 asks you to examine your own voice.

SUGGESTIONS FOR JOURNAL WRITING

1. How would you classify yourself as a writer, experienced or inexperienced or somewhere in between? What about writing do you already know? What else do you want to know?

2. Describe the differences you already perceive between your high school and college learning environments. Explain in what ways you are treated differently by your professors than you were by your high school teachers. Are your reading or writing assignments noticeably different? How so?

3. Which of this chapter's so-called ground rules (for example, that your job as a writer is to create belief) are new to you? On which ones could you elaborate further, with examples from your own experience? Can you add other rules to this list?

SUGGESTIONS FOR ESSAY WRITING

1. Describe your evolution as a writer from some fixed point in time (e.g., third grade or summer camp). Explain how you developed, and identify any milestones along the way.

2. Agree or disagree with one of the ground rules described in this chapter. Support your assertion with as many examples as you can.

3. Imagine and identify a new college discipline. Create a set of ground rules to support it—ground rules that may or may not correspond to those described here. Be imaginative, but persuade us that your new rules make sense.

SUGGESTIONS FOR RESEARCH PROJECTS

1. **INDIVIDUAL:** Locate two or more successful (A or B) papers you wrote for one of your high school courses. (If you're not living at home, you may need to send home for samples.) Examine these papers and ask: Is the writing believable? Does the paper have a serious persuasive intent? Are my assertions supported by evidence? Have I documented all claims? Is my voice relatively subjective or objective (or is it sometimes one, then another)? Do I make any claims that something is absolutely true? Would I call this paper's treatment of the subject balanced?

    See if you can point out words, sentences, or paragraphs where your writing specifically acknowledges or violates these different academic conventions. Write a short paper in which you analyze your own past writing in terms of whether or not it subscribes to the premises of the academic community described in this chapter, being sure to append a photocopy of your original paper(s) to the end of your paper.

2. **COLLABORATIVE:** Think of a discipline that you and some of your classmates are considering for a college major. Examine it as an academic community: which ground rules seem to apply most? To find out more information, some of you look this up in the library while others interview professors in the field. Options: (a) write a collaborative paper or (b) share research but write an individual paper that describes the special ground rules of your possible major. Include full interviews and library sources as appendix material.

Chapter 2

THINKING WITH WRITING

> Writing feels very personal to me. I usually write when I'm under pressure or really bothered by something. Writing down these thoughts takes them out of my mind and puts them in a concrete form that I can look at. Once on paper, most of my thoughts make more sense & I can be more objective about them. Puts things into their true perspective.
>
> [Joan]

A few years ago, I asked my first-year college students to write about their attitudes toward writing. Did they write often? Did they like to write? When did they do it? Why did they do it? For whom? When I read their responses, I was a bit disappointed because all of my students but one said something to the effect that writing was hard for them, that they didn't do it very well, that they didn't like to do it, and that they only wrote in school when they had to for teachers, who graded them. (This last statement seemed to explain a lot about the earlier ones.)

The only exception to this discouraging testimony was Joan, who had stayed out of school for two years and entered my class a little older than her classmates. Joan wrote the paragraph that opens this chapter and, as you can see, valued writing in a different way than the other first-year students. She did not write only to please her teachers. Writing helped her to reflect, to figure things out, and to gain some perspective on thoughts and feelings. This is a valuable way to approach your writing.

USING LANGUAGE

We use language all the time for many reasons. We use it to meet, greet, and persuade people; to ask and answer questions; to pose and solve problems; to argue, explain, explore, and discover; to assert, proclaim, profess, and defend; to express anger, frustration, doubt, and uncertainty; and to find friendship and declare love. In other words, we use language to conduct much of the business of daily life.

When we think of the uses of language, we think primarily of speaking, not writing. We think about speaking first because we do it more often and because it is somehow easier, more available, less studied, more natural. Without being taught, and long before we went to school, we learned to speak. By the time we completed first or second grade, we had also learned both to read and to write. It was in school that we memorized spelling lists, learned to tell nouns from verbs, and diagrammed sentences—none of which we did when we learned to talk. It was in school that we also wrote stories, poems, themes, reports, and examinations, with varying degrees of success. In fact, many of our early associations with writing include school in one way or another.

The farther we advanced in school, the more we were required to write, and the more our writing was criticized and corrected. We wrote more often for grades than for sharing our ideas, for the fun of it, or just for ourselves. For many of us, writing became associated almost exclusively with what we did in school, which was quite different from what we did on weekends, on vacations, for ourselves, or to have a good time.

The purpose of this chapter is to convince you that written language, like spoken, can do many things all the time for various reasons—for ourselves. In fact, the degree to which you understand how writing works *for you* may be the degree to which you succeed in college. To be more specific, let me describe three generally distinctive uses to which you can put your writing: to communicate, to imagine, and to explore.

WRITING TO COMMUNICATE

It is easiest to describe writing as communication because this is the use to which school writing is most obviously put. For years, teachers in elementary, middle, and high school classes admonished you to write clearly, correctly, concisely, and objectively about topics they hoped would interest you. In school they put most of their emphasis on writing; to write clear, correct, concise, objective prose they taught you to use thesis statements, topic sentences, outlines, foot-notes, transitions, and titles, but to avoid cliches, digressions, redun-dancy, and split infinitives. Later, they said, the same principles would be emphasized in your workplace.

In writing to communicate, you probably produced, at one time or another, essays, book reports, lab reports, term papers, five-paragraph themes, and essay-test answers. You most likely spent many hours in school practicing how to use written language to communicate effectively with other people. Of course, much com-municative writing is also imaginative and exploratory, for writing's functions frequently overlap.

WRITING TO IMAGINE

You also spent some time studying, usually in English class, another kind of highly structured language often called "imaginative" or "creative." Poetry, fiction, drama, essay, and song are the genres usu-ally associated with imaginative language. This kind of language tries to do something different from strictly communicative language—something to do with art, beauty, play, emotion, and personal expression—something difficult to define or measure, but often easy to recognize. We sometimes know something is a poem or a play simply by the way it looks on a page, while with a story or essay, we may not.

For example, I could write some language here that you'll read as poetry, largely because of how I make it look:

> Writing to imagine
> Is different from
> Imagining to write
> Isn't it?

But if I simply wrote the sentence, "Writing to imagine is different from imagining to write, isn't it?," you would pay it less attention. Ultimately, it is difficult to describe exactly what makes some writing quite imaginative (a poem by e.e. cummings) and some less so (my lines above).

Poems, novels, and plays are often governed by alternative conventions of language use. Some poets use rhyme (Robert Frost) and some don't (Robert Frost); some fiction writers use conventional sentences and paragraphs (Ernest Hemingway), while others run single sentences through several pages (William Faulkner); most au-thors capitalize and punctuate conventionally, but some don't (e.e. cummings). One glance at this untitled poem by cummings demonstrates an imaginative writer's freedom to violate certain language conventions:

VIII

Buffalo Bill's
defunct
        who used to
        ride a watersmooth-silver
                        stallion
        and break onetwothreefourfive pigeonsjustlikethat
                                Jesus
        he was a handsome man
                        and what i want to know is
        how do you like your blueeyed boy
        Mister Death

In other words, imaginative uses of language often gain effect not only from the ideas about which the authors are writing, but also from the form and style in which those ideas are expressed. In fact, some of the most important elements of imaginative writing may be formal and stylistic; if the author wanted simply to convey an idea clearly and logically, he or she would probably resort to more conventional prose.

WRITING TO EXPLORE

A third kind of writing is that which you do for yourself, which is not directed at any distant audience, and which may not be meant to make any particular impression at all, neither sharply clear nor cleverly aesthetic. This kind of writing might be called "personal," "expressive," or "exploratory." It helps you think and express yourself on paper. You've written this way if you have kept a diary or journal, jotted notes to yourself or to a close friend, or begun a paper with rough drafts that you want to show nobody else. Here is an example of such personal/exploratory writing from one of my composition classes, in which Missy reflects on her experience writing high school papers:

> I was never convinced that it wasn't somehow possibly a
> fluke—like I got lucky & produced a few good papers—that it
> wasn't consistent and that it wasn't a true reflection of my writing
> skills. I felt like this because I didn't know how I wrote those
> damn papers. I had no preset method or formula like you are re-
> quired to have in science. That is why I wasn't convinced. I just sat

down and wrote those papers and w/ a little rework they worked! Presto—now that really baffled me & that is why I thought it was pure chance I turned them out.

This piece of writing is remarkable only in its honesty, but that, of course, is the key feature of writing to yourself—there is no point in pretending. Missy writes in a voice with which she is completely comfortable. In fact, the rhythms of her writing sound as if she is talking to herself on paper: she uses frequent contractions, first-person pronouns (''I''), shortcuts for words (''&'' and ''w/''), and colloquial language (''damn'' and ''Presto'') as if talking to a good friend.

The key feature of this kind of language, spoken or written, is the focus on subject matter as opposed to style or form. When you write to yourself, you concentrate on thoughts, feelings, problems, whatever—and not on an audience. When you write to yourself to figure things out, you use your most available, most comfortable language, which is talky, casual, fragmented, and honest.

This doesn't mean that journals like Missy's need be entirely private, like personal diaries. Actually, Missy wrote this entry in a journal that I asked my students to keep, so she wrote it knowing I might look at it, but knowing also that she could show me only those entries she chose to and that the journal would not be graded. (Class journals will be discussed more specifically in Chapters 4 and 5.)

As an example of a piece of writing written strictly for the writer, I'll share with you a passage from my personal journal in which I wrote about my twelve-year-old daughter:

11/6 Annie is running for student council in her 7th grade class—she's written a speech, a good one, with a platform and all (more options for lunch, etc.). She's rehearsed it over and over—has planned to talk slow and look at just one or two people in her audience to avoid laughing. I'm proud of her—I don't know where she got the idea or guts to do this—but I'm proud of her! She takes it quite seriously—and seems to trust my observations on what she has planned.

I wrote this entry some months ago. As I reread it now, I remember that Annie did not get elected and my heart went out to her. It had been brave of her to run for student council in the first place, and to lose didn't help her fragile twelve-year-old self-confidence. I also remember thinking at the time that it was a harder loss for me, her father, because I realized so clearly the limits of my help and protection: she was really on her own.

So what is the value of having this personal recollection from my journal? At the time I wrote it, while I wrote it, I gave my undivided attention to thinking about my daughter's growing up, something I need to do more of. Now, later, that single recorded thought triggers still more Annie memories: since that time she's begun speaking up more in French class, and she's just had her first boy–girl birthday party (seventeen kids!). And I'm thinking her confidence is in pretty good shape. Quite simply, personal writing such as this increases your awareness of whatever it is you write about.

Another form of personal writing occurs in letters to close friends or people you trust. Such letters reveal your candid, sometimes uncertain, reactions to things; your errant thoughts; and your casual speculations, dreams, and plans. In other words, there are people emotionally close enough to you that writing to them is very much like writing to yourself. In fact, teachers might even turn up in this trusted category. A sixth-grade teacher (Mr. K.) shared with me the following letter written by one of his students after he had talked with his class about alcoholism. He had also given her a magazine article to read.

> Dear Mr. K,
>
> Thank you for the discussion [of drinking] in class. I needed it. I have had a lot of it [alcohol abuse] in my lifetime. The article you gave me "When your child Drinks" I think should be read in front of the class. But it is up to you.
>
> Your friend,
> Marianne
>
> P.S. Your a lifesaver.

I would call this letter a sample of exploratory writing, also, because it is an honest expression of concern to an audience the writer trusts thoroughly. You will notice that neither you nor I was ever intended to read this letter: I had to explain the context of this letter to you (as it was explained to me) so that you would understand the references in it. This is another characteristic of exploratory writing: it isn't intended to go very far away from the writer and thus includes few introductory remarks. The writer (Marianne, an eleven-year-old student) doesn't bother to explain context or elaborate on details to her audience, Mr. K.: they were in class together the previous day and both knew exactly what "the discussion" was about and what "it" refers to.

We have just looked at some samples of exploratory writing in different forms—a class journal, a personal journal, a private letter—and noticed that such writing has common characteristics: it is

(1) centered on ideas important to the writer, (2) honest in judgment, (3) tentative in nature, (4) informal in tone, (5) loose in structure, and (6) not entirely clear to an audience outside the context in which the writing took place. We might note that this writing is bound by few rules; perhaps it should be legible to the writer, but even that is not important in all cases. It simply does not matter what exploratory writing looks like, because its primary audience is the writer (or someone very close to the writer who shares his or her context).

RELATIONSHIPS

Each of the three uses of language we have just explored has a distinct function: to communicate, to create art, and to speculate. In reality, of course, any single piece of writing may have features of the other modes: for example, a piece of writing may be primarily informative but also have aesthetic and personal features. Of the three forms, the most useful for you as a student and learner is the exploratory writing you do to think with. In fact, we could say it is the very matrix from which the communicative and imaginative modes of writing emerge, as we work through possible meanings toward those that we would be willing to share with others.

If, for example, you are assigned a term paper in some course, a good way to begin would be to write to yourself about what you could write about. Do some writing to help you think about doing more writing; but the kind you do first, for yourself, need not be shown to anybody else or graded. In the following example from one of my American Literature classes, Robin works out her impressions and questions about the Edgar Allan Poe story "Descent into the Maelstrom" in her journal before she begins writing the first draft of a critical review paper:

9/13 I have to admit, after reading this story over for the second time, I am still not sure what Poe is trying to tell us. The only thing that even crossed my mind about the whirlpool was, what a fool Poe's companion was not to try some means of escape. Certainly by hanging on continuously to the "ring bolt" he was headed for inevitable death.

Maybe that was one part of what Poe was trying to say, that as life goes on day after day, you can sink into the same routine causing your life to become stagnant and boring. . . . In the story, for example, Poe took the chance of jumping off the boat and hanging onto the barrel—so what could trying something else hurt? Perhaps Poe is also trying to show how fear of death can paralyze a person. . . .

I reproduce Robin's journal entry here because it shows so clearly how a writer must start wherever he or she can to make sense of new information—in this case a story—before being able to write about it for someone else. By admitting her initial confusion, and then going on to speculate about possible interpretations, Robin begins to make sense of the story. The informal writing helps the thinking, which, in turn, helps the formal writing.

WRITING TO LEARN

What all this means in practical terms is simply this: thinking takes place in language, sometimes language that is mathematical, visual, musical, and so on, but most often in everyday words of our native tongue. The degree to which we become fluent, efficient, and comfortable with language as a mode of thinking is, to a large extent, the degree to which we advance as learners.

By writing to ourselves in our own casual voices, we let the writing help us think and even lead our thinking to places we would not have gone had we merely mulled things over in our heads. When you write out your thought, it becomes language with which you can interact, manipulate, extend, critique, or edit. Above all, the discipline of actually writing guarantees that you will push your thought systematically in one direction or another.

The next three chapters examine personal/exploratory writing more thoroughly and suggest how it may help you both to learn and to write better.

SUGGESTIONS FOR JOURNAL WRITING

1. How did you learn to write? Try to recall as much as possible about your use of language in your younger years. Do you remember anything about learning to speak? about learning to write? Why do you think these incidents stand out in your memory today?

2. Make a list of the ways you have used personal writing recently in your life. Did you initiate these uses? How are they important to you?

3. Recall a time that you wrote a poem, story, play, or song and explain why you did it. What was the effect? Did you show it to anybody else? What was your reader's reaction?

SUGGESTIONS FOR ESSAY WRITING

1. Select either a recent experience or something you read. Write one page about this experience or text, deliberately using each of the three modes described in this chapter: communicative (for example, write a letter to someone you don't know especially well), imaginative (try a poem or an imagined dialogue), and personal (honestly, to yourself, as a page in a journal or diary). Was your understanding affected by the mode in which you wrote? Conclude by explaining the effect of each mode on the writer's self.

2. Write a critique or review of this chapter, pointing out places where you agree or disagree with the assertions made. Use your own experience with language to support your position.

SUGGESTIONS FOR RESEARCH PROJECTS

1. **INDIVIDUAL:** Keep track of and list all the writing you do in the course of a normal week: writing checks, letters, shopping lists, examinations, taking notes, even doodling. At the end of the week, divide your list into the three categories we discussed in this chapter—communicative, imaginative, and personal—and determine how much of each kind of writing you did. On the basis of these figures, make a case for altering the teaching of writing in the elementary and secondary schools.

2. **COLLABORATIVE:** As a class or small group, do one of the above exercises, compare notes, and make a similar, more comprehensive case for teaching speech or writing differently.

Chapter 3

WRITING TO SOLVE PROBLEMS

I am divided about where to go right now. I was interested in researching the "airport expansion" but now I'm not sure. The history of the Church Street Mall sounds really interesting—I think there is more information on that. (I haven't really looked for information on either one.) My first problem is deciding between the two. If I decided on the airport, I would probably have to go to the Newspaper and look up a lot of articles. Going toward the mall I would first have to narrow down my subject. But if I did the airport I could also find out how many people used the airport, when it was built. . . . If I went downtown I could go to the mayor's office. . . .

[Betsy]

Betsy's problem is what to write about. We don't know from this entry what her solution will be, but it's apparent that she's willing to let the writing help her decide. No matter whether you're trying to figure out what to write about in an English class, trying to solve a chemical equation, or grappling with something much more personal such as whether to switch majors—the act of writing is one of the most powerful problem-solving tools humans have at their disposal. (By the way, Betsy decided not to write about either the airport or the mall; instead she chose to write about "Champ: The Lake Champlain Monster," which shows that part of problem solving is deciding which problems you don't want to solve.)

Writing works to help us solve problems in at least two different ways. On the one hand, it makes our thoughts visible, allowing us to expand, contract, modify, or discard them. We can hold only so many thoughts in our heads at one time; when we talk out loud and have dialogues with friends, or with ourselves, we lose much of what we say because it isn't written down. More importantly, we can't extend, expand, or develop our ideas fully because we can't *see* them. When we can witness our thoughts, we can do something with them.

On the other hand, the act of writing itself generates entirely new thoughts that we can then further manipulate. Writing one word, one sentence, one paragraph suggests still other words, sentences, and paragraphs. Writing progresses as an act of discovery; no other thinking process helps us so completely develop a line of inquiry or a mode of thought. Scientists, artists, mathematicians, lawyers, engineers all "think" with pen to paper, chalk to blackboard, hands on terminal keys. Extended thought about complex matters is seldom possible, for most of us, any other way.

In this chapter we will look at some of the specific ways that writing helps people find solutions to problems and answers to questions.

ASKING QUESTIONS

To solve a problem, you need to identify it. In the example that opened the chapter, we saw a first-year writer asking herself questions on paper to determine which problem—the airport or the mall—she really wanted to investigate further. One of the best methods of problem solving is simply trying to identify exactly which problem you need or want to solve.

A colleague of mine teaches chemistry to classes of two hundred students. Because this large class doesn't easily allow students to raise their hands to ask questions, the instructor has asked the students to write out their questions during the lecture and deposit them in a cardboard box labeled QUESTIONS that sits just inside the doorway to the classroom. At the beginning of the next class period, the instructor answers selected questions before moving on to new material. A few of the questions from the chemistry question box are reproduced here exactly as they were found, demonstrating how sometimes writing out the question can actually lead to the answer.

A fairly typical question from a fairly confused student is given in Figure 3-1. In this example, there is no evidence that in writing out this question the student is one whit closer to finding an answer than when he or she started, which, of course, will often be the case. But consider the next question (Figure 3-2). In this example, the student writes out a question that he or she takes a stab at answering at the same time: "Is sulfur an exception?" The instructor read this ques-

Figure 3-1

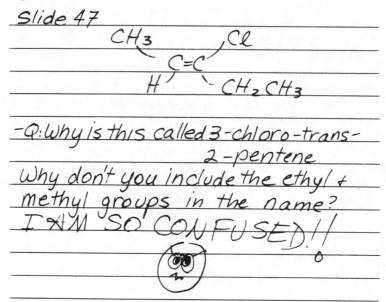

Slide 47

-Q: Why is this called 3-chloro-trans-
                    2-pentene
Why don't you include the ethyl +
methyl groups in the name?
I ~~AM~~ SO CONFUSED!!

Figure 3-2

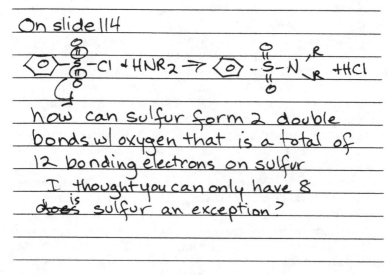

On slide 114

how can sulfur form 2 double
bonds w/ oxygen that is a total of
12 bonding electrons on sulfur
    I thought you can only have 8
~~does~~ is sulfur an exception?

tion to the class and simply answered "yes" as the student was actually ahead of the lectures at this point.

Now look at the next example (Figure 3-3). Here the student began to ask a question during lecture, and in the process of writing out the question, figured out the answer. (We have this sample only because other unanswered questions were written on the same scrap of paper.)

In the last example (Figure 3-4) a similar process is at work. This student not only realizes that "the peptide bond" is the answer to the question, but decides to share the discovery with the instructor to thank him, apparently, for the opportunity of asking questions in the questions in the box in the first place.

The principle at work in the last two examples is a powerful one: the act of saying how and where one is stuck or confused is itself a liberating process. It is unclear exactly why this happens or how to guarantee that it will continue to occur, but I suspect that we've all had similar experiences, both in speech and in writing.

The next time you are confused about a math problem or the lines of a difficult poem, try to write out the precise nature of the confusion. It is possible that in articulating your question you will

Figure 3-3

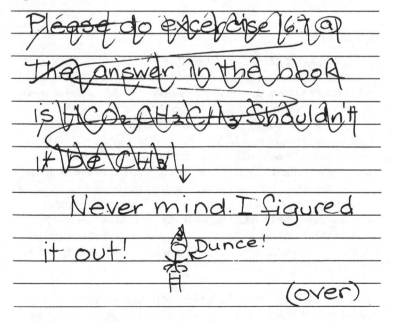

Figure 3-4

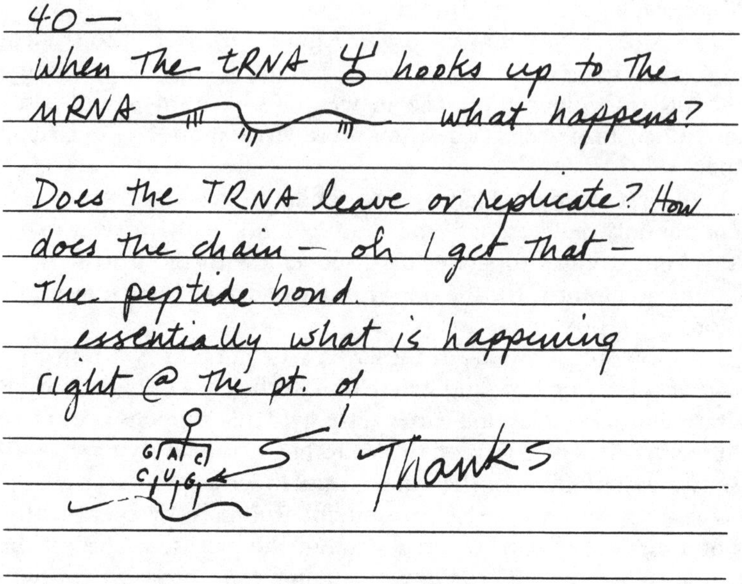

find your answer, but if not, at least you will have a clear statement of the question from which to begin a more methodical quest for an answer.

FREEWRITING

Freewriting is fast writing—likethis—about anything that comes to mind—as fast as you can do it & without worrying about what it looks like at all—just trying desperately to write as fast as you can think—as I am now—not worrying at all about what the words look like, trying rather to catch the flow of thought on my mind—which right now IS freewriting & so I write here as fast as I can for a fixed period of time (for me I usually write from 5 to 10 minutes at a crack, then back off & look at what I've wrought—writ—whatever). I don't freewrite well on the typewriter because I make so many typing mistakes—wihch distravct me—and so I usually freewrite by hand either in my journal or on a scratch pad. In this sample I've gone back and fixed most of the typing mistakes—otherwise you'd spend more time deciphering it than I did writing it.

Freewriting is a powerful problem-solving tool. Ignore it at your peril! Writing fast helps you in two distinct ways. First, freewriting is a good way to start any piece of writing; the technique forces you to write on, instead of stare at, a blank piece of paper (or a blank computer screen). You stop trying to decide *how* to start and just start. When you freewrite, you just start and don't worry about where it's going or what, exactly, the words look like at this particular time. If it turns out that what you've written is important, you'll go back later and make it look nice; if it has been a stimulus to one or two good ideas, you'll copy those and go on from there; if nothing interesting happened, you'll just throw it away and maybe try another one.

Freewriting also helps because it turns off your internal editor and insists that you write out the very first word/thought that occurs to you, much like the exercise of free association, where in response to a prompt ("black," for example) you say the first word that comes to mind ("white"?). The benefits to a thinker, problem solver, or writer—at least during initial stages of writing—are substantial, because if you can avoid editing your thought before it comes out, you have more to look at, play with, modify, and expand. During these initial phases of problem solving, it's more important to see variety and quantity than development and quality. Freewriting helps spread out the problem for examination.

It doesn't matter whether you use freewriting as a technique to find out what's on your mind, to address a specific issue that puzzles you, or to start composing a formal paper. It's an all-purpose generative activity and, as such, is transportable to many different situations.

The directions for freewriting are quite simple: (1) write fast; keep your pen moving; (2) use whatever shortcuts you like ("&" for "and") and don't worry about spelling, punctuation, and the like; (3) let the words chart your thinking path (which means digressing is just fine); (4) write for a fixed period of time (ten minutes works well); and (5) if you can't think of anything to write, write "I can't think of anything to write" until you do.

Of course, techniques such as freewriting do not work for everyone. One of my students, Sean, wrote the following passage in his journal:

> I'm not sure that this rapid fire methodology helps me. I need to look over my work. Scratch it out. Curse at it. Scream. Cry. And all those other things that make me a writer.

I tried to convince Sean that he could write fast sometimes and go back and do the more careful stuff later, but he was never comfortable with freewriting, and I didn't push it. Different techniques work for different people.

(If you want more information on freewriting, consult either of these highly readable books: Ken Macrorie's *Telling Writing* [Portsmouth, NH: Boynton/Cook, 1970] or Peter Elbow's *Writing Without Teachers* [New York: Oxford University Press, 1973].)

CONCEPTUAL MAPPING

Writing doesn't always look like writing. I find that many times when I'm trying to figure something out, I'll write single words or short phrases on a sheet of paper, circle or put boxes around them, then connect these to one another with lines or arrows. In fact, I use this shorthand "visual writing" more than any other kind when I'm trying to delimit a problem or think about a freewriting topic. Sometimes I do this on empty journal pages, other times on restaurant place mats—whatever is handy.

Here is one concrete example: If for any reason you need to break a problem or question down into manageable size—say to make a presentation about the Vietnam War or locate the best marketing strategy for a hypothetical business venture—consider making a quick visual map to see what the problem territory looks like. Start by writing out your general topic area (for example, Vietnam War) in the center of a sheet of paper and put a circle around it. Then you see how many possibilities you can think of and cluster them around your central idea in smaller circles, as in Figure 3-5.

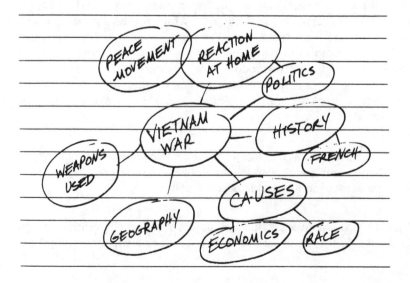

At this point you may have already found the issue you want to investigate, in which case you can continue using this technique to refine your topic, your next circled word being "Causes of the Vietnam War," and so forth.

If you want to discuss a number of the issues you have just diagrammed, you might put priority numbers next to the various circled terms. In the Vietnam War example, we might enumerate these subtopics to explore further: (1) history, (2) politics, (3) reaction at home. This list then becomes the beginning of an outline into which to add still more detail, or it becomes an order of investigation on your part. The point is that the visual spread of ideas helps you both to see relationships and to discover new possibilities, and it does so even more rapidly than freewriting.

(Two of the best books on the use of visual language as an aid to writing and problem solving are Gabriele Rico's *Writing the Natural Way* [Los Angeles: Tarcher, 1983] and Linda Flower's *Problem Solving Strategies for Writing* [New York: Harcourt Brace Jovanovich, 1981].)

LIST MAKING

People make lists every day to remind them of projects to do, things to buy, errands to run. Most obviously, when you make a list of grocery items, you have a record to consult in the store. Equally important, however, in starting the list is the power of the list itself to generate useful associations and new thoughts: you write "eggs" and think also about bacon; you write "milk" and remind yourself of other products in the dairy case, etc. The same thing works with the lists I make in my journal or appointment book to remind myself of what I need to do today, this week, before vacation, etc. By writing the list I remind, remember, and create a visual display of ideas to mull over and modify.

I make lists all the time both to jog my memory and to suggest new possibilities. I make lists when I have a problem to think about, project to develop, article to write, lecture to prepare. Moreover, I often revise those lists to see what else is possible. For instance, to create a class syllabus, I often start with a list of authors—Twain, James, Crane, Frost, Eliot, Dickinson, Melville—then add, subtract, and rearrange until I like the logic of the course before me. To write this book, I started with a list of three chapters, later expanded to twenty, and finally cut it to the eighteen you are now reading.

After I have an idea I like, I often start with another list to see (1) where else that idea could go, (2) what its dimensions are, (3) the pro arguments I can think of, (4) the con, and (5) how many organizational sections the paper might have. Even *this* list is not exhaustive; I arbitrarily decided to find five examples—the list could just as easily have numbered four or twelve.

Writers and thinkers of all kinds use lists to initiate and continue developing a piece of writing. Instead of settling for the first idea that pops into mind for that narrative English paper or history research report, write it down and see what other possibilities exist. In this sense, list making is like an abbreviated freewriting exercise or a conceptual map; the same principles are at work.

OUTLINES

Outlines are organized lists. After you have decided what to write about (what problem to solve), an outline can give you a clear direction, a goal toward which to write. To make an outline, you list ideas according to their relative weight: some ideas are equal to others (coordinate), and other ideas are supportive of larger ideas (subordinate). In formal outlines, broad coordinate ideas are designated with Roman numerals, and related supportive ideas are clustered beneath larger ideas, with progressive indenting from there. Here, for example, is an outline for this chapter:

USE OF WRITING TO SOLVE PROBLEMS

    INTRODUCTION

        I. ASKING QUESTIONS
           A. CHEMISTRY EXAMPLE #1
           B. CHEM #2
           C. CHEM #3
           D. CHEM #4

       II. FREEWRITING
           A. DIRECTIONS FOR DOING
           B. HOW IT HELPS
              1. Starting
              2. Continuing
                 a. free association
                 b. focusing

      III. VISUAL THINKING [etc.]

      IV. LIST MAKING

       V. OUTLINING

      VI. BRAINSTORMING

     VII. ROLE-PLAYING

I have decided to discuss outlining here as a problem-sólving tool rather than discuss it somewhere else as a more formal part of writing. For me, outlines are always generative; that is, I use them in the formative stages of determining what to write and where to direct my writing. And while I do use Roman numerals and capital letters on occasion, my outline usually is a series of words or phrases arranged and rearranged to show relationship and direction. I seldom take an outline to the detail shown above; once I'm close to where I want to be, I start writing. I believe outlines are important in that they let me think through a project roughly before actually beginning it, but I never hold a writing project to the outline that helped originate it because I see outlines—like freewrites, maps, and lists—as planning, not governing, activities.

Where outlines prove especially useful is in long projects such as books, reports, and grant proposals, in which it is important that readers receive a map, a table of contents, to help them through the long written document; in essence, a table of contents *is* an outline of the work, allowing both writer and reader to find their way.

BRAINSTORMING

Professional problem-solving groups in government and corporate think tanks alike use the power of lists to help them do an activity called "brainstorming." Here's how it works: a group of seven to fifteen people gets together for an hour to focus on solving a particular problem. Each member writes privately for five or ten minutes to focus on the problem. Then a leader asks the group to suggest possible solutions as rapidly as possible, while someone writes the ideas on a flip chart or blackboard for all to see. Participants are encouraged to say anything that comes to mind, no matter how wild or crazy sounding, on the belief that the wild idea may stimulate someone else to think of something more practical.

During this entire intense session, nobody is allowed to make any negative criticism of anybody's ideas—again to keep the focus as positive and productive as possible. The leader will often use goals to stimulate even more rapid thinking: "We've got forty-one ideas now. Can we hit fifty?" Later, at another session, the revision and editing begins, as the long wild list is pared down to a few good ideas. (If you want to know more about brainstorming, read Alexander Osborne's *Applied Imagination* [New York: Charles Scribner's Sons, 1953].)

The principles at work are similar to those in freewriting or visual thinking, but in brainstorming you are using other people to help the generation and association. In a classroom setting or among friends, it would be easy to duplicate informally some of the power of collective brainstorming; on paper, by yourself, making lists is based on the same ideas of association and generation.

Brainstorming simply takes the power of list making and pushes it even harder. Next time you make a list to find options for something, see how long you can make it—push yourself to see if you can come up with ten ideas. The pushing to reach some arbitrary goal sometimes generates your best ideas: if you had stopped at #8 you'd never have found #9, which proves to be your best idea!

ROLE-PLAYING

When you adopt a role in writing, you also gain a problem-solving edge. For example, if you have to write a paper in which you are given a fair amount of latitude, writing from a role will give you (and your reader) a new slant on the topic.

Here are some examples of what I mean. (1) Recreate Henry David Thoreau's "lost chapter" in *Walden*. (2) Write a paper on the Civil War from the perspective of a recently emancipated slave—or a southern planter after General Sherman passed by. (3) Develop an argument against Plato's *Republic* from Aristotle's perspective. (4) Recreate a debate (or a series of letters) between psychologist B. F. Skinner and anthropologist Margaret Mead on whether human behavior is determined by environment or heredity.

My point is simply that the necessity of examining a situation through someone else's eyes allows you, the thinker/writer, to see the situation differently—and what helps you see differently helps you find new solutions to problems, in writing and otherwise.

In the next two chapters I'll explore journals as systematic ways of posing and solving problems, asking and answering questions.

SUGGESTIONS FOR JOURNAL WRITING

1. Detail some of the strategies you have used in the past to solve problems. Which have been the most successful? Why so?

2. Describe one time when you were stuck trying to figure something out and you had that "Aha!" experience like the chemistry student in Figure 3–4. What circumstances helped create this insight?

3. Think about one problem—personal or academic—you are currently trying to solve, and explore it, using at least two of the modes—freewriting, mapping, listing, etc.—discussed in this chapter.

SUGGESTIONS FOR ESSAY WRITING

1. Describe the greatest problem—in life or school—that you remember solving. Explain, if you can, the role language (talking or writing) played in identifying or solving the problem. (To begin this assignment, use one or more of the problem-solving strategies described in this chapter; append a sample of this to your completed paper.)

2. Think about one thing you are especially good at, such as a sport or hobby, and describe the kinds of problems you encounter in this sport (learning how to spin the ball in table tennis?) or hobby (finding a particular CD for your jazz collection?). Explain how you go about solving those problems—what do you do first? next? how does the solution arrive?

SUGGESTIONS FOR RESEARCH PROJECTS

1. **INDIVIDUAL:** Conduct a library search on the literature of problem solving and create a bibliography of what you find. Write a report in which you describe the use of problem-solving strategies in a field that especially interests you.

2. **COLLABORATIVE OR INDIVIDUAL:** In addition to (or instead of) searching the library, conduct interviews with people who work in a particular field or discipline and ask them about how they identify and solve problems. Divide up the interview tasks, but share the results and write (or orally report) about the problem-solving strategies in the field you investigated.

Chapter 4

THE WRITER'S JOURNAL

9/7   Perhaps this journal will teach me as much about myself as it will
      about English. You know, I've never kept a journal or such before.
      I never knew what a pleasure it is to write. It is a type of cleansing
      almost a washing of the mind . . . a concrete look at the workings
      of my own head. That is the idea I like most. The journal allows me
      to watch my thoughts develop yet, at the same time, it allows me a
      certain degree of hindsight.

[Peter]

In this passage, Peter describes journals well when he calls them
places "to watch [his] thoughts develop" and to allow him a "certain
degree of hindsight." Journals are collections of thoughts, impressions, musings, meditations, notes, doubts, plans, and intentions
caught chronologically on paper. You write them for yourself in your
most comfortable language.

In this chapter I want to share some of the journal entries I have
photocopied from student journals (with student permission) over
the last few years. Many of them came from the classes I teach in
composition and American literature, but a fair number were given to
me by colleagues in other disciplines, including botany, philosophy,
political science, mathematics, and history. These samples suggest
what is possible with journal writing. For the most part, they are
interesting samples; I have seen many others much less interesting for
outsiders to read, although they may have served their authors well.

OBSERVATIONS

In a small loose-leaf notebook, Mary describes the ideas she finds in reading the essay "The American Scholar" by Ralph Waldo Emerson:

9/25 In the first few paragraphs of this address, Emerson seems discouraged at the way society is run, that there are no "whole men" left . . .

     . . . He seems to feel that scholars should learn from books, but he says beware that you don't become a "bookworm." Use the books to inspire your own thoughts, <u>not</u> to copy the thoughts of others.

Mary is a first-year student enrolled in literature class, and she is using her journal to "observe" more carefully what she reads by writing about it. Notice, especially, that she copies direct quotations from what she reads, key phrases that she will remember better because she has written them out. These observations become particularly useful to her the next day when these essays are discussed in class; they are also useful later when she studies for her final examinations.

In a spiral notebook, Alice, a biology major, describes what she sees happening in the petri dishes containing fern spores:

9/5 Well, first day of checking the spores. From random observation it seems that the Christmas Fern is much less dense than the Braun's Holly Fern.

Alice makes the following notations amidst other data describing what she sees in each of the 20 petri dishes she is monitoring as part of her senior thesis project:

1a nothing
2a an alive creature swimming around a pile of junk
3a looks like one spore has a rhizoid
4a one spore has a large protrusion (rhizoid beginning?)

In a science class, students commonly keep something like a lab or field notebook in which they both collect and speculate about data. This, too, is a kind of journal—a daily record of observations, speculations, questions, and doubts. Whether you are observing the words in books or the spores in petri dishes, the journal helps you look, remember, and understand.

DEFINITIONS

Journals are good places to ask yourself questions about what you are doing with specific assignments, in specific courses, and in your major. In the following entries, we see students in several different disciplines trying to define or explain to themselves what, exactly, their fields of study are really about.

4/24 What makes politics scientific? How is it related to other disciplines? What tools do political scientists depend on most? Is it really a discipline by itself or does it need to be combined with other disciplines (i.e., the social sciences)? This is a hard subject to write about.

[Oscar]

5/2 Sociologists study groups for various reasons. They teach us to recognize how a group functions, how to seek out and influence the leaders, how to direct and control the masses. There are questions of ethics raised. It is taught as a process. The process is all-important. . . . Taking apart a jigsaw puzzle, sociologists learn to unravel and identify distinct parts of the process.

[Marc]

3/7 Unlike math, where you must learn how to add and subtract before you can multiply and divide, philosophy is a smattering of different things with no exact and precise starting place. In philosophy we could start anywhere and end up anywhere without ever having gone anywhere, but we would have uncovered many rocks along the way. Ah Hah! This is our task: uncovering rocks along the way.

[Doug]

On one level, it simply helps to put any concept or term into your own words to try to make sense of it in language you understand. Each of the writers here writes his or her own definition and so increases the chances of truly understanding the concept.

In addition, as we become immersed in our own disciplines, we begin to take too much for granted. Sometimes your instructors stop questioning, at least in public, the basic assumptions around which their disciplines are actually built—assumptions that need periodic re-examining if the disciplines are to remain healthy. Journals are good places in which to ask yourself why you are studying what.

CONFUSION

Journals are good places to write about what you don't understand, where you are having trouble, and where you are confused. Sometimes writing about that which doesn't make sense helps it make sense; sometimes just the venting helps. In the following entry, Mary is venting her frustration about reading Emerson's "American Scholar" essay:

> 9/22 Of course, I'm not a scholar, but if I had to sit and listen to a speech like this I wouldn't be able to figure out what the heck he is talking about. Even after reading it for the third time I still can't figure out half of what he's saying.

This is the same Mary who wrote thoughtfully about this same Emerson essay in the earlier section "Observations." Mary wrote this entry about three days before she slowed down and looked at the essay more carefully. The act of writing out your frustrations actually helps you focus on them and deal with them productively. In Mary's case, the fact that she earmarked the Emerson essay as difficult made her work harder to understand it—which eventually she did.

SPECULATIONS

One of the best uses for a journal is speculating on the meaning of what you are studying and thinking about. Speculating is essentially making attempts at answers that you are not yet sure of. Speculating on exams or papers is dangerous; doing it in journals is natural. In the following entry, one of my literature students speculates on the meaning of a well-known passage in Henry David Thoreau's *Walden*:

> 10/24 What really caught my attention was the specific description of the fight between the black and red ants. In this chapter is Thoreau trying to put his friends (the wild animals) on the same line as those people in the village?

Bill's question, which poses an answer, is a good one. The more he speculates on the meaning of the various passages in *Walden*, or any other book in any other subject, the more ideas he will have to discuss in class and the more material about which to write further papers or exams. The speculation in his journal could lead to further investigation into other places where Thoreau makes similar comparisons (see Chapter 14 on Research Logs).

INSIGHTS

One of the most exciting things that happens while you're writing in journals is stumbling onto important thoughts in the act of writing. You usually can't *see* this happening, but sometimes you can. When Missy was working on a report for my composition class the semester before she was to graduate, she wrote this passage:

> 3/12 (after class) Look, we botanists don't ask "Does that plant exist?" and we don't ask about the aesthetic value of a flower. We ask "What is the economic value of this plant?" But that is not the primary interest of a true botanist.
>
> We want to know why it grows there (ecologists), why a plant has the structure it does (evolutionist), how it does its stuff (physiologist), etc. The discipline of botany has excluded lots of other questions and that is why I'm having some problems with it. . . . Yikes! I think it's all coming together!

Missy doesn't explain for us exactly what she sees coming together, but then she isn't writing for us either. She is using the journal to think through some important issues that concern her now that she's about to become a professional botanist; in fact, she was using a lot of her composition journal to wrestle with matters closer to botany than English. This is exactly what a journal is for: talking with yourself about the issues that concern you most deeply. Sometimes it even seems to answer back.

CONNECTIONS

Use your journal to find connections deliberately. Make as many as you can in any direction that works. Connect to your personal life, connect to other courses, connect one part of your course to another. In the following entries Kevin works on connections in a course on macroeconomics:

> 2/16 One of the things about this course seems to be the fact that many theories can be proved algebraically. For example, the teacher said that a possible exam question might be to trace through a Keynesian model. In order to trace it one has to use a lot of algebra, substituting variables inside certain functions to prove equations . . . by explaining it this way you get a better grasp of things . . . economics becomes less ambiguous. Theories backed up by mathematical, algebraic, or statistical evidence always seem much more concrete.

2/26 It [economics] is beginning to pull together. After reading the chapters for the second time, I'm beginning to see a sequence or passage of ideas from chapter to chapter.

Of course, if you read the material twice, review your notes, and keep a journal, connections are bound to happen. In Kevin's case, he is pulling it together, and the journal is a helpful part of this process.

RESPONSES TO READING

A colleague of mine who teaches the History of Science asks his students questions about their reading that are to be answered in their journals. He enjoys it when students write entries such as the following:

#17   What did Darwin find on the Galapagos Islands? Lions & tigers & bears? Oh no. Turtles & lizards & seals! That's what he found. Different from species found anywhere else in the world. Tame and unafraid of humans. Adapted to a harsh isolated environment. The birds, such as the woodpecker thrush, had learned to use tools. No other species, except man and baboons, I think, had learned to use tools. Some birds had no more use for flight so their wings atrophied.

Journals are places in which to have some fun with language—to amuse both yourself and your instructor (if you like). This entry is fun to read while still full of good specific information about Darwin.

When I teach my literature classes, I tell students "Write about everything you read in here, even if just for five minutes. Whenever you complete a chapter, a poem, an essay, write something, anything, about it in your journal. Date your entry and try to identify something specific in what you are reacting to." By making this assignment I am hoping to make writing about reading a habit. If you write about what you read, you increase your chances of remembering it, understanding it, and asking intelligent, specific questions about it. A first-year literature student wrote the following entries while reading *Moby Dick*:

11/30 The thought of running into that squid makes me sick. Don't these men get scared of these strange creatures? Nobody can be that strong all the time.

12/1 What I thought was funny is that Stubbs calls the ship they meet the Rosebud and it is giving off a gross odor because of all the sick and dying whales it carries. What's even more humorous is that the ambergris (yellow substance) is used in perfume—it comes from the bowels of dying whales!

The more personal Sarah's reaction, the more I believe that she is engaged in the book; the more she discovers that she finds funny or notable, the more likely she could use that entry as a seed from which to start an analytic essay or research project.

REACTIONS TO CLASS

Journals are not the place for class notes, which are frequently mere copies of teacher's thoughts, but they are good places in which to evaluate what took place in class, to record your opinion of the worth of the lecture or points made by classmates during a discussion. In the following entry, Caroline, a senior English major, comments on her Shakespeare class:

2/9   In Shakepeare class today I was aware of my fellow students and
        wondered what each one of us was thinking—about the class in
        general, about the professor, about each other's comments, about
        Shakespeare. I could sense and see that some students were there
        only in body. Some of them obviously hadn't read Hamlet, many
        hadn't even brought their books to class. I felt they had closed
        themselves to literature—What, in contrast, makes me care about
        these plays?

Caroline's candid reaction to class will inevitably help her remember both the form and substance of that particular class meeting better than if she had not written about it. Repeated entries such as this would be likely to sharpen her powers of observation and depth of understanding as well.

SELF-AWARENESS

Writing in journals promotes more awareness about whatever it is you are writing about, be it history, economics, literature, or the act of writing itself. Use your journal to examine your attitudes toward ideas, class, or simply the act of writing. After a few weeks of keeping a journal in his first-year writing class, Kurt wrote:

9/28 I am really amazed at myself! I don't ever recall writing this much
        in my life—especially in a journal. I write down a lot of ideas I get,
        I write in it when a class is boring (usually chemistry lecture) and

I write in it because I want to. It helps me get things off my chest that are bothering me.

Kurt's reaction is fairly typical of students who are starting to get serious about some elements of college (not necessarily chemistry) and are finding the journal a useful companion in advancing their thought—sometimes to their own surprise.

CONVERSATIONS

If your teacher asks to collect and read your journal, then you have a good chance to initiate some dialogue in writing about things that concern you both. Journals used this way take on many of the qualities of letters, with correspondents keeping in touch through the writing. As a writing teacher, I have learned a great deal about my own teaching from written conversations with my students.

Remember Alice, the biology major studying the fern spores in the petri dishes? Her professor responded to nearly every one of her observations, briefly, to let her know if she was on the right track. At midpoint in her project, her professor wrote the following:

10/15 Here are some questions designed to organize your thoughts in groups: (1) What interspecific interactions are promoted? (2) What intraspecific interactions are promoted? (3) What about the experimental design casts doubt on your inferences about interactions?

I don't understand these questions, and you probably don't either, but in the context of Alice's project journal, they made complete sense. In journals you can carry on virtually private, closed, tutorial-like conversations with your instructor, even if he or she never asked you to keep one. Sharing journal entries is more like sharing letters than any other kind of writing you are likely to do in college.

REFERENCE

Journals are also good places in which to review, revise, and actually reference your thoughts. Because they represent a progressive and cumulative record, you are bound to evolve perspectives on material and ideas that differ from earlier perspectives you wrote down. In addition, as your course progresses and you switch from one topic to the next, your tentative summations of material can prove to be valuable reference points. In fact, I suggest making it a regular habit to summarize your current thought *and* review your previous thought. In the following entry, John writes about the value of his math "workbook," essentially a journal kept for a mathematics class, as a useful personal reference document:

> Well, I take back everything bad I ever said about keeping a workbook. . . . What I like most about my workbook is that it is a source of reference. When I forget a concept I can look it up. I usually know exactly where to look because my workbook is a very personal thing. My workbook also shows my growth and progress in linear algebra . . . all my homework can be found in one place and in a very neat and efficient order.

John's workbook was an especially careful production, with sections clearly labeled with different problem-solving strategies. Such a workbook is clearly a hybrid between a class notebook and a journal, a combination that seemed to suit his purpose for studying mathematics.

EVALUATIONS

Your journal may also prove to be a good place in which to reflect on the value of journals themselves. I no longer believe journals work for everyone—some people just don't like to be reflective in language— but as course assignments go, they are fairly painless. Let me conclude with some of Jim's observations; he started keeping a journal in my first-year writing class with some reluctance; later he wrote the following on page 192 of his journal:

> 11/11 As I scan through my journal, I found a lot of memories. I wrote consistently on my classes and found grades to be one of my big hang-ups. . . . The entries which helped me the most were those about myself and my immediate surroundings. They helped me to realize who I am. Maybe I should say what I am. I have a little bit of everyone inside of me. . . .
>
> I really enjoyed looking back to see what I wrote. Some entries were stupid. . . . Many times I wrote what I really felt. A journal wouldn't be worth keeping if I didn't. Who wants to read about what other's think? Never once did I feel it a burden to write. If you would have told us to write in it everyday, I would have told you where to go. My roommate says I write too much, but I think I write too little.

I have presented these examples from college student journals in a variety of grades and disciplines to make the case that journal writing can be among the most important writing you do in the academic world. It *is* the language of thought written down. In the next chapter, I will describe some of the particular strategies that will make journals work in easily among your other college assignments.

SUGGESTIONS FOR JOURNAL WRITING

1. Describe any attempt you have made in the past to keep a journal, diary, log, or methodical notebook of any kind. What were the results? Why did you start? stop (if you did)?

2. For one week, focus on one dimension of journal writing that you normally ignore (e.g., observation or evaluations) and write as many entries that do this as you can. (And, of course, write a journal entry about the results.)

3. Think of five good questions to do journal entries about for this class you are now taking. (Consider, for example, the subject you are studying this week, how the class is run, what today's discussion was about, what frustrates or excites you.) Share these, if the occasion presents itself, with your teacher and classmates.

SUGGESTIONS FOR ESSAY WRITING

1. For two weeks, keep a journal in another class you are taking (use the back part of the class notebook). During this time, try to make as many entries as you can of an exploratory or questioning nature, about both the class and the readings. After two weeks, write an evaluation of the two-week journal-keeping experiment.

2. Keep a reading journal about a book you are currently reading. When you have finished, examine the pros and cons of writing while reading, including in your essay any passages from your actual journal that may support your case. (Append a sample of your journal to the end of this paper.)

3. Keep a journal for the duration of one research project or paper you are doing in another class. When the project or paper is finished, edit and write an introduction to this journal in which you explain its role in finishing the product. (Append the finished paper to the journal for reference.)

SUGGESTIONS FOR RESEARCH PROJECTS

1. **INDIVIDUAL:** Locate in the library the published journal of somebody who interests you. (Journals I have looked at include

Leonardo da Vinci, Anaïs Nin, C. Wright Mills, Edward Weston, and Henry David Thoreau.) Write a report in which you explain, if you can, how this journal was related to his or her life or work.

2. **COLLABORATIVE:** Interview some of your teachers or other working people in your community who keep something like a journal. Find out why they keep it, how they use it, and how often they write in it. Put together a report for this class on what you have learned from this research about informal modes of writing.

Chapter 5

JOURNAL WRITING: HOW TO

3/17 The dynamics of this journal are sort of wierd. I've kept a personal
  journal on & off since I was in 5th grade—sometimes consistently
  writing daily entries as I did in Norway—sometimes not writing a
  word for months. But it has always been a personal need & has
  never been written thinking someone will read it . . . except myself in 50 years when I'm curious enough to be reminded of the
  person I was at 22.

    So I don't know—this journal now being kept for a specific
  class as a specific assignment to be handed in! How do I deal with
  this?! Certainly there are pages that will come out, but even so,
  overall I feel unsure. So many of my entries are semi-personal (?)
  Is this emphasis wrong? . . . What is personal? What is appropriate?

[Missy]

Missy, a senior majoring in botany, enrolled in my composition class
to sharpen her writing skills before she graduated. I asked her to keep
a journal to become more aware of herself, her world, and her
writing. From the start, she used her journal to ask good questions. In
this passage, she wonders about the possibility of keeping a journal
that's meaningful to her but shared with me, her instructor.

    If you are asked to keep a journal for a class, the chances are that
your teacher wants it to focus on his or her course. Like me, other
teachers assign journals, hoping to increase your understanding of the
goals, readings, lectures, and discussions that compose this class in
composition or literature or history or biology. Such a journal will be

useful to the extent that you maintain the focus on the course content and, at the same time, write honestly and personally about that content.

If you elect to keep a journal on your own and not because a teacher asked you to, bear in mind that it will be useful to you only if you write in it regularly and candidly about problems and insights that really concern you. Assigning yourself a journal—for one class in particular or your whole academic term in general—is a good idea because it is the one writing assignment that works for you more than for someone else.

In this chapter I want to explore how you can make a journal work for you, whether or not you are required to keep one. I want to answer Missy's questions with a series of compromise suggestions. There is no formula for what a journal should look like, how it should be kept, or what it should contain. In fact, what I am calling journals have traditionally gone by many other names, including logs, learning logs, daybooks, workbooks, thinkbooks, notebooks, field notebooks, laboratory notebooks, and diaries.

JOURNALS, LOGS, NOTEBOOKS, AND DIARIES

The informal notebooks that collect your personal thoughts have a long and respected history. Documents like journals or diaries or notebooks have existed ever since people discovered that writing things down helped people remember them better. For travelers and explorers, the journal was the place to document where they had been and what they had seen. Some of these journals, such as those by William Byrd and William Bradford in the seventeenth century, are especially useful for modern historians in reconstructing a portrait of the settlement of colonial America—as are *The Journals of Lewis and Clark* about the settlement of the west in the early nineteenth century.

Some writers, like James Boswell, wrote journals full of information about other famous people—in Boswell's case, Samuel Johnson. Other writers, such as Ralph Waldo Emerson and Virginia Woolf, kept journals that contained nearly all the germinal ideas and language for their later published manuscripts. And the notebooks of Dostoyevsky and Kafka provide crucial insights into the disturbed personalities of these disturbing writers.

Many famous literary figures, of course, kept journals; some became more widely read than anything else they wrote. For example, Samuel Pepys' *Diary* remains one of the liveliest accounts of everyday life in seventeenth-century London, and Anaïs Nin's *Diaries* (all four volumes), which describe life in mid-twentieth-century Paris, have contributed more to her fame than have any of her other works.

Other creative people have depended on journals to locate, explore, and capture their ideas. In the journal of Leonardo da Vinci, we find a wonderful mix of artistic and scientific explorations, including both sketches and words. Painter Edgar Degas' notebooks of visual thoughts acted as his journal. Photographer Edward Weston's "daybooks" explored all manner of his personal and aesthetic life in Carmel, California, in the 1920s and 1930s. Le Corbusier's *Sketchbooks* document in detail the emergence of his architectural ideas.

We gain numerous insights through the published journals of noteworthy people. In Charles Darwin's diaries, written aboard the HMS Beagle, we witness the evolution of the theory of evolution. In B. F. Skinner's journals, we locate the rational mind of the father of behaviorism. And in the diaries of Arthur Bremer and Lee Harvey Oswald, we witness the twisted minds of political assassins.

If you want to explore the many possibilities of journal writing, you might investigate one of these published journals in an area that interests you. It would certainly give you some ideas about keeping one yourself. The rest of this chapter provides guidelines for keeping journals in academic communities.

ACADEMIC JOURNALS

When you keep a journal for a college or university class, it's a good idea to avoid the extremes: the personal diary and the impersonal notebook. At the one extreme you find diaries, which are private accounts of a writer's thoughts and feelings and which may include more writing about emotion than intellect. At the other extreme are documents such as class notebooks, which are usually meant to be impersonal recordings of information and other people's ideas. I would diagram the differences this way:

DIARY ----------------------JOURNAL ----------------------CLASS NOTEBOOK
[I-centered]   [I/subject]   [subject-centered]

But even the opposite ends of the spectrum are related: both are regular, often daily, records of people writing primarily to themselves about things that concern them. For academic purposes, I would suggest a judicious blend of both diary and class notebook, taking from the diary the crucial first-person pronoun "I" (as in "I think" and "I wonder") and taking from the notebook the focus on a given subject matter (English, history, political science). Write from the perspective of what you think about and how you react to English, history, political science. If your teachers assign journals, it is quite likely that this is where their interest lies.

SUGGESTIONS FOR KEEPING JOURNALS

The following suggestions have proved useful to students enrolled in my literature and composition classes. They are, however, only a few of the many available possibilities. For every one suggestion here I can think of a dozen variations that may work equally well. If you have a good method for keeping your own journal, stick with it. If you haven't successfully tried a journal before, these suggestions may help.

1. Buy a loose-leaf notebook. The special advantage of a loose-leaf over a bound notebook is the ease with which you can add, subtract, and rearrange your writing. With a loose-leaf notebook, you can share portions of your journal with someone else—your teacher or classmates, for example—but keep on writing. If you write a highly personal entry in a school journal, you can simply withhold it when the teacher asks to read your entries and restore it later. I prefer small thin notebooks, about 7 by 10 inches, because they are easily carried in book bag, knapsack, or briefcase; other teachers prefer 8½- by 11-inch notebooks because standard handouts can be inserted along with one's journal entries.

2. Divide your notebook/journal into sections. In my own journal I have two sections: the first for personal entries about my life, family, friends, goals, dreams, and ambitions; the second for professional notes about books and articles I have read or am writing myself. During the year, when I am teaching, I'll have additional sections for each class. I would recommend a similar approach for students: keep one part of your journal for private thoughts, another for each class you are taking. If a teacher wants to look at your journal entries, pull out those entries from his or her class, clip them together, and hand them in—leaving the rest of your journal for you to continue writing in.

3. Date each entry. Your journal will become a record of your thoughts extended through time; the dates will document the distance between one idea and the next, and later will help you see the very evolution of your thought. In my journal I also jot down the time of day, place, and some-

times the weather, quick references that ground my writing/
my life.

4. Start each entry on a new page. I do this to provide a good
   length of page to work with, to remind me that the longer I
   write the better my chances of finding something interesting to say. I also like the white spaces this method leaves in
   my journal, because I then have room to add later notes or
   occasional clippings.

5. Write in your natural voice, your most comfortable language. In journals, you want to write in the language that is
   easiest for you to use, that requires the least attention as you
   write. Otherwise, you may become distracted by form
   rather than content—and that's a mistake. Journals are
   places to worry ideas into shape; worry your language into
   shape when you write formal essays.

6. Write with your favorite pen. This is not, of course, a
   commandment—none of these suggestions is—but I would
   try to make writing in your journal something special, and
   writing with a favorite pen often helps that. I actually use
   an old fountain pen, preferring the nice lines of black ink it
   lays down to those of ball points and felt tips. (Some journal
   keepers prefer to type entries, using loose-leaf pages for
   later insertion.)

7. Write at the same time and at different times of the day.
   Writing in the morning finds me rather on task, making
   plans, lists of things to accomplish during the day, and the
   like; writing late at night finds me in a more reflective
   mood, looking inward, writing more emotionally. I find
   both moods for writing valuable, just different.

8. Write in the same place and in different places. Here too, I
   like to write in certain places that I know will be quiet and
   comfortable: on my front porch, back deck, in airplanes. I
   also find that writing in different places causes some different thoughts: on the beach, at a shopping mall, in a
   dentist's waiting room.

9. Write regularly. I don't necessarily mean daily. Theoretically, I intend to write daily, more likely, I write four or five
   times a week—although sometimes two or three times on a
   given day. When writing becomes habit, you will find it an
   easier and more versatile tool for problem solving and self-
   reflection both.

10. Prepare your journal for public reading. This advice per-
    tains to journals assigned by teachers for specific courses. In
    such cases where your journal has a definite beginning,

middle, and end, I would recommend that, prior to final submission, you put in page numbers, a title for each entry, a table of contents, an introduction, and a conclusion. This act of final ordering is a review for you and a wonderful courtesy to your reader, showing the seriousness with which you have taken the assignment.

We will now leave the relative privacy of journal writing and move on to writing directed at more public audiences. However, I'm convinced that all successful writing is grounded first in personal knowledge and understanding. I wouldn't leave my journal very far behind.

SUGGESTIONS FOR JOURNAL WRITING

1. Write about one suggestion for keeping journals that strikes you as especially interesting or that you've never tried, and why you think it may be useful to you. Then try it.

2. Write about one suggestion with which you're already familiar or that you've tried before: How did it work?

3. Write deliberately in different styles (e.g., with no capitalization, long and complex sentences, and short and abrupt ones) for a while: Is it clear that one is easier and more natural than another?

SUGGESTIONS FOR ESSAY WRITING

1. Make a case for the value of a journal in another class you're now taking, especially one in which journals seem unlikely assignments. Write this as a letter or report and give it to your teacher.

2. Examine your own journal going back two or three weeks and create a profile of the person you find there, using as evidence what you find in the journal. (If you haven't written very much, try this assignment a little later in the term.)

SUGGESTIONS FOR RESEARCH WRITING

1. **INDIVIDUAL:** In the library, find the journal of one of the journal keepers mentioned in this chapter. Compare this published journal to your own in any way that proves fruitful.

2. **COLLABORATIVE:** Everyone in the class make a photocopy of one journal entry written during the past several weeks, an entry

you especially enjoy or that you think is especially stimulating. Put these together in one volume, and share and discuss the many ways in which journals are being used among your classmates and yourself.

Part II

WRITING
FOR READERS

Chapter 6

THE ROLE OF AUDIENCES

> For me, in most cases, I'm writing because I have to, not because I want to. . . . I'm usually writing for a grade, it puts on more pressure. Most of the time people communicate through talking. Talking is more natural, you can read other people's expressions—it's easier to sense if you're right or wrong.
>
> [First-year college student, anonymous]

Many jobs in business, government, and education involve writing for different audiences. In the course of daily business, you may write memos to co-workers, letters to complete strangers, reports to your boss, and notes to yourself. Even if you've never been required to write at work, you probably learned about audience expectations simply by having written for various teachers in passing from one grade to the next in school, and by writing letters to friends and parents, and thank-you notes to aunts, uncles, and grandparents. In fact, most of us had already learned to distinguish one audience from another before we learned to read or write, as we used oral language to communicate with different people.

WRITING AND TALKING

Most of us would agree with the writer above who believes that talking is easier than writing. For one thing, most of us talk more often than we write—usually many times in the course of a single day—and so get more practice. For another, we get more help from people to whom we speak face to face than from those to whom we write. We see by their facial expressions whether or not listeners understand us, need more or less information, or are pleased with our words. Our own facial and body expressions help us communicate as well. Finally, our listening audiences tend to be more tolerant of the way we talk than our reading audiences are of the way we write: nobody sees my spelling or punctuation when I talk, and nobody calls me on the carpet when, in casual conversation, I blow an occasional noun–verb agreement or mis-use the subjunctive (whatever that is).

However, writing does certain things better than speaking. If you miswrite, you can always rewrite and catch your mistake before someone else notices it. If you need to develop a complex argument, writing affords you the time and space to do so. If you want your words to have the force of law, you can make a permanent (written) record to be reread and studied in your absence. And if you want to maintain a certain tone or coolness of demeanor, this can be accomplished more easily in writing than in face-to-face confrontations.

Because most readers of this book are likely to be students, we will look at some of the audiences for whom students most commonly write and see what help is to be had.

WRITING FOR TEACHERS

When you are a student in high school, college, or graduate school, your most common audiences are teachers who have requested a written assignment and who will read and grade what you produce. But teachers are an especially tough audience for most of us.

First, teachers often make writing assignments with the specific intention to measure and grade you on the basis of what you write. Second, teachers often think it their civic duty to correct every language miscue you make, no matter how small. Third, teachers often ask you to write about subjects you have no particular interest in—or worse, to write about *their* favorite topics! Finally, your teachers usually know more about the subject of your paper than you do because they are the experts in the field, which puts you in a difficult spot: you end up writing to *prove* how much you know more than to share something new with them.

You can't do much about the fact that teachers will use your writing to evaluate you in one way or another—they view it as part of their job, just as they do when making assignments "for your own good" (but not necessarily interest). However, as an individual writer, you can make choices that will influence this difficult audience positively—especially if you understand that most of your instructors are fundamentally caring people.

In the best circumstances, instructors will make writing assignments that give you a good start. They do this when they make clear their expectations for each assignment, when they provide sufficient time for you to accomplish the assignment, when they give you positive and pointed feedback while you are writing, when they create a climate in which it's clear that the subject belongs to *you*, not to them or the text or the school, and when they evaluate your papers according to criteria you both understand and agree with.

But regardless of how helpful you find your teacher, at some point you have to plan and write the paper using the best resources *you* can muster. Even before you begin to write—or as you think about the assignment through writing about it—you can make some important mental decisions that will make your actual drafting of most assignments easier:

1. Read the assignment directions carefully before you begin to write. Pay particular attention to instruction words such as "explain," "define," or "evaluate"—terms that mean something quite different from one another. (See Chapter 8 for more information on instruction words.) Most of the time when teachers develop their assignments, they are looking to see not only that you can demonstrate what you know, think logically, and write clearly—they also want to see if you can follow directions.

2. Convince yourself that you are interested in writing this assignment. It's better, of course, if you really *are* interested in writing about *Moby Dick* or the War of 1812 or photosynthesis, but sometimes this isn't the case. If not, you've got to practice some psychology on yourself because it's difficult to write well when you are bored. Use whatever strategies usually work for you, but if those fail, try this: locate the most popular treatment of the subject you can find, perhaps in a current newsstand or by using the *Reader's Guide to Periodical Literature*. Find out what has made this subject newsworthy, tell a friend about it (Did you know that . . .?), write in your journal about it, and see what kind of questions you can generate. There is a good chance that this forced engagement will lead to the real thing.

3. Make the assignment your own. This can be done by any of the following methods: (a) recasting the paper topic in your own words, (b) reducing the size/scope of the topic to something manageable, or (c) relating it to an issue with which you are already familiar. Modifying a writing task into something both interesting and manageable dramatically increases

your chances of making the writing less superficial because you're not biting off more than you can chew and because the reader will read caring and commitment between the lines.

4. Try to teach your readers something. At the least, try actually to communicate with them. Seeing your task as instructional puts you in the driver's seat and gets you out of the passive mode of writing to fulfill somebody else's expectations. In truth, teachers are delighted when a student paper teaches them something they didn't already know; it breaks the boredom of reading papers that are simple regurgitations of course information.

5. Look for a different slant. Teachers get awfully tired of the same approach to every assignment, so, if you are able, approach your topic from an unpredictable angle. Be sure you cover all the necessary territory that you would if you wrote a more predictable paper, but hold your reader's attention by viewing the terrain somehow differently: locating the thesis in *Moby Dick* from the whale's point of view; explaining the War of 1812 through a series of dispatches to the London *Times* from a British war correspondent; describing photosynthesis through a series of simulated field notebooks. (I provide these examples only to allude to what may be possible; teacher, subject, and context will give you safer guidelines.)

6. Consider your paper as a problem in need of solution or a question in need of an answer. The best way to start may be to try to write out in one sentence what the problem or question actually is, and to continue with this method as more information begins to reshape your initial formulation. For example, the question behind this chapter is: What is the role of audience in writing? The chapter itself is an attempt at answering. (The advice of my high school math teacher to help solve equations may be helpful here: What am I given? What do I need to know?) Approaching it this way may help you limit the topic, keep your focus as you both research and write, and find both a thesis and a conclusion.

7. View the paper topic from your teacher's perspective. Ask yourself how completing this paper helps further course goals. Is it strictly an extra-credit project in which anything goes? Or does the paper's completion also complete your understanding of the course?

Each of these ideas suggests that you can do certain things psychologically to set up and gain control of your writing from the outset. Sometimes none of these suggestions will work, and the whole process will simply be a struggle; it happens to me in my writing work more often than I care to recount. But often one or two of these ideas will help you get started in the right direction. In addition, of course, it helps to consult the teacher with some of your emerging ideas. Because the teacher made the assignment, he or she can best comment on the appropriateness of your choices.

WRITING TO CLASSMATES

Next to the teacher, your most probable school audience is your peers. More and more teachers are finding value in asking students to read each other's writing, both in draft stages and in final form. You will probably be asked to share your writing with other students in a writing class, where both composing and critiquing papers are everybody's business. Don't be surprised if your history or biology teacher asks you to do the same thing. But equally important to remember is that you could initiate such sharing yourself, regardless of whether your teacher suggests it; the benefits will be worth it.

Writing to other students and reading their work is distinctly different from simply talking to each other; written communication demands a precision and clarity that oral communication does not. When you share your writing with a peer, you will be most aware of where your language is pretentious or your argument stretched too thin. If you ask for feedback, an honest classmate will give it to you— before your teacher has to. I think that students see pomp and padding as readily as teachers do and are equally put off by it. What's the point in writing pretentiously to a classmate?

The following are some of the possible ways to make sharing drafts profitable:

1. Choose people you trust and respect to read your draft. Offer to read theirs in return. Set aside enough time (over coffee in the snack bar?) to return drafts and explain your responses thoroughly to each other.

2. When possible, *you* decide when your draft is ready to share. I don't want someone to see a draft too early because I already know how I am going to continue to fix it; other times, when I am far along in the process, I don't want a response that suggests that I start all over. There's a balance here: it's better that I seek help on the draft before I become too fond of it, when I tend to get defensive and to resist good ideas that might otherwise help me.

3. Ask for specific responses on early drafts. Do you want an overall reaction? Do you have a question about a specific

section of your paper? Do you want help with a particularly intricate argument? Do you want simple editing or proof-reading help? When you share a draft and specify the help you want, you stay in control of the process and lessen the risk of your reader's saying something about your text that could make you defensive. (I'm very thin-skinned about my writing—I could lose confidence fast if I shared my writing with nonsupportive people who said anything they felt like about my work.)

4. When you comment on someone else's paper, use a pencil and be gentle. Remember how you feel about red ink (bad associations offset the advantages of the contrasting color), and remember that ink is permanent. Most writers can't help but see their writing as an extension of themselves. Writing in erasable pencil *suggests* rather than *commands* that changes *might* rather than *must* be made. The choice to do so remains where it should, with the writer rather than the reader.

5. Ask a friend with good language skills to proofread your paper before submission. Most readers can identify problems in correctness, clarity, and meaning more easily in another person's work than in their own. When students read and respond to (or critique) each other's writing, they learn to identify problems in style, punctuation, and evidence that may occur in their own writing.

PUBLICATION

Writing for publication is something you may not have to do while you're still in school. Conversely, you may have already done so in letters to the newspaper editor or articles for a school paper. However, you may have a teacher who wants you to experience writing for an audience that doesn't know who you are. When you write for an absent audience, there are a few things to keep in mind:

1. Assume ignorance unless you know otherwise. If you assume your audience knows little or nothing about what you are writing, you will be more likely to give full explanations of terms, concepts, and acronyms. Because you will never know exactly into whose hands your published piece will fall, it's always better to over- than to under-explain. (This suggestion, of course, is also a good one to use for known academic audiences. The cost of elaborating is your time; the cost of assuming too much will be a lower grade.)

2. Provide a full context that makes it clear why you are writ-

ing. This is true in books, articles, reviews, and letters to the editor. You can often do this in a few sentences early in your piece, or you can provide a footnote or endnote. Again, no harm is done if you provide a little extra information, but there is a real loss to your reader if you do not.

3. Examine the tone, style, and format of the publisher before you send your manuscript. You can learn a lot about the voice to assume—or avoid—by looking at the nature of other pieces published in this medium.

4. Use the clearest and simplest language you can. I want to be careful here not to be prescriptive, because the level of language you choose is dependent on your analysis of the situation in which you're writing. However, I would not try overly hard to sound erudite, urbane, or worldly; too often the result is pretension, pomposity, or confusion. Instead, let your most comfortable voice work for you, and you'll increase your chances of genuinely communicating with your reader.

5. If you are worried about having your manuscript accepted, send a letter of inquiry to see what kind of encouragement the editor gives you. This gives you a better indication of what the editor wants; it also familiarizes him or her with your name, increasing your chances of a good reading.

YOURSELF

One more audience is especially worth commenting on: yourself. Regardless of your intended audience, you, too, must be pleased with your writing. You want it to represent you well. You want just the right combination of thought and expression to create just the right impression. Our first audience is always ourselves. We must think our own writing "good."

In exploratory writing, your focus is primarily on your ideas (see Chapters 1 through 5). But when you write for a teacher, classmate, or editor, you are most likely to please them when you please yourself first. The following suggestions may help you do that:

1. Read aloud to yourself from your own writing. Listen to the rhythms of your words and sentences: Do you like them? Do they sound natural or forced? (If you are a native speaker of English, your ear should tell you these things. If you are not, read them to a native speaker for a reaction.)

2. Edit. Allow time to reread your finished paper, looking for repetitions, inexact explanations, imprecise words, useless words, and clear-cut mistakes.

3. Proofread. The last act of editing is proofreading to catch typos and simple errors. Because I write on a computer that has a program to check my spelling, I use that first. But that won't catch mistaken correct spellings ("their" for "there"), typos that accidentally create correct words ("do" for "so"), usage or punctuation mistakes, or omitted words. In the end, I must proofread the old-fashioned way, reading slowly, moving a ruler down line by line, forcing myself to read every word.

Writing to different audiences will be a fact of your working life, whether you are in business, engineering, law, medicine, politics, teaching, foreign service, etc. Those of you who excel at it may well get the early promotions. You will learn to do it, one way or another, when you have to. Why not start now?

SUGGESTIONS FOR JOURNAL WRITING

1. Are you more confident of your language ability as a writer or a speaker? (Don't settle for a simple response here; examine yourself in various settings and see if your answer is always the same. To what extent does your answer depend upon circumstances? How so?)

2. For whom do you write most often: a friend? a parent? a teacher? yourself? Explain how you write differently to this person than to anybody else.

3. Who is the toughest audience for whom you've ever had to write? What made him or her so difficult? Would this difficulty still exist today?

SUGGESTIONS FOR ESSAY WRITING

1. Write a short paper or letter to three distinctly different audiences. (Make these *real* so that you actually keep an individual in mind as you write.) Sandwich these three papers in between an "introduction," in which you explain the context of each paper, and a "conclusion," in which you explain how and why your language varies from one audience to another. (I'm assuming you do change your language, in major or minor ways, as you change your audience; if not, I wonder if you're really keeping unique audiences in mind when you write?)

2. Choose one assignment that you have already written a paper for in one of your classes—this or another class—and reshape it as a

short article for your school newspaper. Before you do this, make observations in your journal about what changes you intend to make and, after completing it, what changes you actually did make.

SUGGESTIONS FOR RESEARCH PROJECTS

1. **INDIVIDUAL:** Select a topic about which you would like to know something more. Locate one or two sources of information (from the library or other people) and take good notes. As a class, identify a bunch of arbitrary (interesting, different, unusual) audiences; write one per slip of paper and place in a hat; each student draw an audience out of a hat; each write briefly (1–2 pages) to this audience. (Results could be read and evaluated by playing the same game in reverse, with different students role-playing these different audiences for each other.)

2. **COLLABORATIVE:** Interview teachers, professors, or other published writers in your community and ask how thinking about audiences affects their writing. Prepare a collaborative report in which each student writes up one interview. (These could be short, separate chapters in a booklike publication.) Two students volunteer to edit and write an introduction to the collection. As a whole class, list the several conclusions about audiences that might be drawn as a result of this project. Append this list to the collection as a conclusion.

Chapter 7

WRITING FROM EXPERIENCE

10/19 When I write a paper, I inevitably make it personal. I put myself
into it and I write well. I'm paranoid when people criticize it because they tell me to make it more impersonal—to take me out of
it. I'm afraid I can't write unless I am in the paper somehow. . . .
I guess I feel defensive because this paper has so much of me in it
that I'm just laying myself open to all kinds of attacks, and I'm
scared to read it to someone. I want to take it to [my teacher] tomorrow and ask him what he thinks. . . . What I want badly is
for him to say it is a really good paper—but I won't believe him. I
think it's good. But if he's looking for an analytical paper I may
as well forget it. . . . If someone says I should rewrite it, make it
less informal, I'd die inside and give up.

[Jody]

Writing about your personal experience is risky. You invite your
readers in and show them what's in your life and hope that they'll like
what they find. Or, if they don't, that they'll at least tell you so gently.
In the journal entry here, Jody describes this fear quite well. Later she
came to talk to me about her paper. I think she went away from our
talk feeling relieved, not to mention alive.

Figuratively, at least, writers find ideas to write about in one of
two places: inside or outside. The inside ideas come from people's
own memories, imaginations, and insights, aspects of the self
uniquely one's own. The outside ideas come from books, people,
objects, and events. (Never mind that what's inside was once out or

that what's outside has to, at some point, come in.) To write about personal experience, writers go inside, retrieving impressions, images, and words buried somewhere in their memories; from these resources writers create personal narratives, informal essays, autobiographies, and a variety of personal manifestoes.

To write about something unfamiliar, where memory has no stock of stored information, writers must go elsewhere—to additional reading, fresh observation, or new research. From these resources stem much of the writing we call academic—term papers, critical essays, laboratory reports—as well as most of the writing in the working world.

Of course, categorizing all writing as either inside or outside is too simplistic. Many serious writers mix and match sources of information—some with greater abandon than others—so that few pieces of writing are strictly one category or the other. No one can remember *everything* that happened in even one simple experience, and others who were there will remember it differently.

Writers fill the gaps in their memories by reading newspapers, talking to other people, inventing dialogue, fabricating description, and revisiting places in which experiences occurred. Likewise, in writing research reports, authors may draw on remembered ideas, associations, and events; current insights; as well as books, interviews, and observations.

To further complicate the matter, some writers also search their minds to imagine and create *what never happened or existed*; we call this kind of writing imaginative, creative, fictive, or poetic. Poets and novelists, of course, are the greatest mixers and matchers of all, having "poetic" license to move freely from memory to library to imagination in a single page, paragraph, or sentence. The reader should note that while strictly imaginary writing is outside the scope of this book, the lines between the imagined and the remembered are often blurred.

A good example of the mix of inside/outside sources in a single essay can be found in one of Annie Dillard's short personal narratives, "Living Like Weasels,"* which is based on her encounter with a weasel in the woods. Look at the mix of sources she draws on in these six short samples taken within a few pages of one another:

1. She leads with a statement and a question:

   A weasel is wild. Who knows what he thinks?

---

* *Teaching a Stone to Talk* (New York: Harper & Row, 1982), pp. 12–16.

2. She explains the context of the essay:

> I have been reading about weasels because I saw one last week. I startled a weasel who startled me, and we exchanged a long glance.

3. She describes the weasel both literally and figuratively:

> Weasel! I'd never seen one wild before. He was ten inches long, thin as a curve, a muscled ribbon, brown as fruitwood, soft-furred, alert.

4. She retells a story from a book about weasels:

> And once, says Ernest Thompson Seton, once a man shot an eagle out of the sky. He examined the eagle and found the dry skull of a weasel fixed by the jaws to his throat. The supposition is that the eagle had pounced on the weasel and the weasel had swiveled and bit as instinct taught him, tooth to neck, and nearly won.

5. She questions and imagines on the basis of her reading:

> I would like to have seen that eagle from the air a few weeks or months before he was shot: was the whole weasel still attached to his feathered throat, a fur pendant? Or did the eagle eat what he could reach, gutting the living weasel with his talons before his breast, bending his beak, cleaning the beautiful airborne bones?

6. She speculates about the meaning of life:

> I think it would be well, and proper, and obedient, and pure, to grasp your one necessity and not let it go, to dangle from it limp wherever it takes you. . . . Seize it and let it seize you up aloft even, till your eyes burn out and drop; let your musky flesh fall off in shreds, and let your very bones unhinge and scatter, loosened over fields . . . from any height at all, from as high as eagles.

In rapid succession, the essay writer has wondered, explained, described, researched, questioned, imagined, and speculated about a single personal experience. In so doing, she has made that experience rich, multidimensional, and full of potential meaning about herself, the weasel, their encounter, the world.

In this chapter we'll look at writing that draws primarily on a writer's personal experience, narratives, and autobiographies. In subsequent chapters we'll look at writing that depends on other sources to create belief: expository essays (Chapter 8), interpretive essays

(Chapter 9), set pieces (Chapter 10), imaginative writing (Chapter 11), and research papers (Chapters 13 through 17).

PERSONAL NARRATIVES

> **narrative:** n. the general term for a story long or short; of the past, present, or future; factual or imagined; told for any purpose; and with or without much detail.

You are most likely to write personal narratives—that is, writing based on more truth than fiction—in composition courses where your awareness of yourself (where you came from, how you got here, what you believe and why) is often central to your further development as a writer. However, you may sometimes write in the personal narrative mode in another discipline that emphasizes self-knowledge, such as psychology, philosophy, religion, education, art, or nursing. Writing a personal narrative implies that you tell some story about yourself, about something that happened in your life or that you witnessed. This experience should be one that has meaning for you, or something you would be willing to explore to find meaning.

In the process of such self-exploration, writers often search their memories and reconstruct believable stories with beginnings, middles, and ends. Some personal narrative writing assumes the first-person point of view ("I"), uses simple past tense ("Last summer I worked at McDonald's"), and is organized chronologically. Other narrative may be told from an objective point of view ("Last summer *he* worked at McDonald's") or mix chronology (starting in the present and working backward). And, of course, still other narrative includes much of the writing in novels and short stories, an enormously rich, complex category we won't attempt to deal with in this book.

Narrative writing includes elements long familiar to all of us. *Description* fills in concrete detail, sets scenes, and allows readers to "see" the events narrated. *Dialogue* provides a sense of the dramatic, the present moment realized, and allows readers to witness people and situations crucial to the narrative. *Exposition* explains what's going on and helps readers keep abreast of the narrative action. In other words, writing from and about personal experience asks you to draw on many of the same writing skills useful in writing critical essays and research papers.

For the remainder of this chapter we'll look at some of the qualities of narrative writing and see what we can borrow for our own writing.

Subject

Inexperienced writers sometimes assume that they have to write about something dramatic or sensational to interest readers: the afternoon I scored the winning touchdown, the night I danced the Sugar Plum Fairy role in *The Nutcracker Suite*, or the morning I nearly died drag racing my father's Porsche. I'd like to suggest that some of the strongest narratives often result from taking something less significant—even disappointing—that happened to you and making it come to life for your reader. Instead of the big touchdown, how about the game you sat out on the bench? Instead of the dance performance, how about dance rehearsal? Instead of near-death in the Porsche, how about your near-death, one day, from boredom? What I'm suggesting, of course, is to take something fairly common and make something uncommon out of it, which sometimes focuses on the disappointing or tedious moments of life.

Recently, I asked the twenty-two freshmen in my writing class to write narratives about topics of their choice. As you might guess, they wrote about nearly everything: high school sports, the first day at college, the death of a grandfather, the divorce of parents, childhood games, travel to Florida, record collecting, moving to a new city, a mother–daughter relationship, and a number of work experiences.

For the moment, let's look at six papers. Five dealt with jobs, the sixth with a judo class the writer attended. Jobs prove to be fertile narrative topics because most students have worked at something and enjoy swapping stories about it. Most of these students, however, didn't write about the drama of their experience—there seemed to be little of that—but about the everyday nature of it. Let me give you some idea about their subjects by showing you their lead paragraphs.

> JOAN: I was a Dunkin' Donuts girl. Just another face behind a pink hat and a grease-stained uniform. The job could have been degrading if I ever let it get under my skin. To get the job I had to be able to count out a dollar's worth of change and read . . .
>
> JEFF: The heat from the huge multiple amplifiers drains every bit of energy out of me. The sweat from my body soaks my uniform right through, like I fell into water. It's dripping into my eyes, burning them because it's mixed with sulfuric oxide. My safety glasses are constantly slipping to the end of my nose . . . None of these precautions do any good because I'm wet with sweat in 150-degree heat, waiting like a target to be shocked . . .

SUE: Every morning when I woke up, the dull throbbing of my lower back reminded me that I worked the night before. The odor of stale cigarettes, French onion soup, and grease from the grill lingered in my room, coming from my uniform crumpled on the floor . . .

FRANK: I never really minded running around, it was just so monotonous. The life of a gopher could be summed up in a few short commands: "Hand me that! Pick up these! Help me with this!"

STEPHANY: T.G.I.T. Thank God It's Tuesday. I always look forward to Tuesdays. They mean two things: Tomorrow is my day off and today is my boss's day off, so I won't be asked to pick eggs. I really hate picking eggs—I get all covered with dust, eggs, and grain. By the end of the day I'm so tired I just want to sack out. When I was hired my boss told me I'd only have to pick eggs once in a while, but this week I had to pick three times. It really gets me, because my real job is candling eggs.

KATE: "Ten pushups? You've got to be kidding!" I don't think I've ever done more than two in my life. I strain my arms trying to touch the mat . . .

It's not the subject, of course, but the treatment that draws us in or turns us away. In these examples, Joan's bouncy opening reminds us more of a cheerleader than a coffee shop waitress, and we wonder what else lies ahead. Jeff starts fast, giving us little context, except to see him drenched in sweat on the battery assembly line waiting to be electrocuted (do we read on, in part, to see how he survives?). Sue describes her job from the morning after; Frank describes his with the words of his many bosses as he helps lay underground cable; Stephany's colloquial, talky voice carries us into her piece; Kate's present tense puts us with her on the mat doing warm-up exercises.

Some of these writers, such as Kate and Jeff, wrote their opening paragraph on the first draft and let it stand through successive revisions; others, such as Stephany, found this opening only in the last draft. And one, Joan, scrapped the strong opening printed here for a different approach in subsequent draft (see Chapter 11 for what she eventually wrote). In short, each writer had to work through his or her own process to find the writing that was most satisfying.

Time

One of the most difficult problems of writing narrative or autobiography is deciding how much time to spend on what. A common mistake is trying to cover some great expanse of time, often resulting in diluted generalizations: my summer job at McDonald's all seventy-four days of it; or how I learned karate, starting with my life as a ninety-pound weakling. Instead of trying to cover such vast periods in a few pages, writers are likely to benefit when they focus sharply in time and space. Instead of trying to generalize about all summer at McDonald's, how about one hot day behind the hamburger grill? Or one afternoon? Or one hour?

Ironically, the smaller the focus in time, the more you will find to say. You really can't say much about a generic day or generic hamburger grill, but you can say something truly substantial about that humid Thursday in August when you worked the grill on your own for the first time.

Look again at the paragraphs describing the students' jobs, and you will notice how several begin quickly by putting you right there, at a specific spot on a specific day: in the battery factory, at the egg farm, on the judo mat. We re-experience these particular places with the writers and feel as if we're present, on the spot, glimpsing into a real and private world—that's what makes us read on. Strong narrative makes us relive an experience with a writer and adds to our own store of vicarious experiences.

Don't misunderstand: great narratives have been written that cover great expanses of time; others offer outrageous generalizations. Nevertheless, for most writers most of the time, specificity is the key to creating belief.

Belief

There are few rules to follow when writing narrative, but the writing that works best for me portrays a chunk of experience and makes me *believe* that this really happened, this is *true*.

Being honest as a writer and creating belief for the reader may be slightly different. Many writers of personal narrative believe that they must stick only to precisely remembered, detailed fact. ("I can't include that detail because I'm not sure of exactly what I said, and I don't remember what I was wearing.") Keep in mind, however, that writing a nonfiction narrative about something that happened in your life will not result in an exact report of what really happened; you will omit some details, select only certain facts, forget some emotions, and misremember more than you realize. No matter how hard you try to get it right, you will distort, modify, and, in effect, *lie*. It is unavoidable. Writing can represent reality; it can never replicate it.

The trick is to remember as best you can and be willing to *recreate* to fill gaps. If you don't remember exactly what you said, you might recreate dialogue that is approximate, typical of you, close to what you might have said; if you don't remember the exact shoes you wore on that hot Thursday, you might remember shoes you could have worn, and what they looked like and how they felt. If this sounds devious, consider that we do it all the time when we tell oral stories. Of course, how you create belief is often through the careful use of pertinent detail.

Detail

As a writer, you can make your narrative believable in several ways. In the following examples, our student writers convince us that they are telling the truth by providing concrete detail, precise action, appropriate language, honest emotion, and documentable facts.

1. Inside knowledge. Readers like to be let into worlds that they have seen only from the outside. Often the small details let them in. In the following passage, Sue shows us what she knows as an experienced filler of salad bars:

   > I could fill three crocks in one trip, unless it was something messy like beets or applesauce. It took time to refill those because they splashed.

   In the next passage, Stephany, who worked summers on an egg farm, teaches us about a job few of us knew existed, candling eggs:

   > Candling is easy. All you have to do is take four flats of somebody's eggs and spin a hundred of them in front of a bright light to look for cracks. Then I count the number of cracked eggs and write it down on my candling sheet next to the egg picker's name.

2. Action. Narrative writing includes action that convinces us the writer has been where he or she claims to have been. Here, Kate describes her judo instructor's demonstration of a hold in class:

   > He grabs the student around the neck, holding the head tight with the elbow and shoulder. The extended arm is pulled in and the instructor also holds it in position. As the student struggles to get free of the hold, it only tightens.

3. Authentic language. Convincing narrative shows us people talking in rhythms of speech that sound believable. In the following passage, Kathy recreates her first day working at a supermarket, and we can hear her talking:

> I can't believe it, I actually started work at Wilson's today—my first job! They hired me as a cashier, but now they tell me I'll be bagging and keeping the strawberry bin full, at least for a while. I guess they want me to become familiar with their system and working with people before they train me to run a register.

4. Emotion. Feelings are part of remembered experience. In the following passage, Bobby describes both his own and his father's emotion in a tension-filled automobile:

> "I can hardly see the road, it's raining so hard!" my father yelled. . . . Sensing the nervous frustration in my father's voice, I felt a chill that came from knowing that my cool, calm, collected father was in a state of panic.

In the next example, Joan recreates her disillusionment about her job at the donut shop through understatement; we can hear her feelings between the lines:

> The thrill of this job is gradually wearing off. I guess I still haven't gotten over the incident with Mr. Stacy. I'm on the night shift now, 6 p.m. until 2 or 3 a.m., so I don't see him much. He usually calls a few times during the night to ask how many customers are there and how much money I've made, but stays home.

5. Facts and figures. Narrative often gains in credibility the same way that more objective writing does, with believable data. Jeff has conducted research about the battery factory in which he has worked and, at one point, tells us the following:

> With 16 manufacturing plants and 5,800 employees, Johnson Controls is the largest of 5 major competitors in the country.

6. Figurative language. Narrative is often strengthened when the writer makes a telling analogy, simile, or metaphor that makes us "see" the story more vividly (remember Annie Dillard's weasel "thin as a curve, a muscled ribbon"?). In the following example, Paul, who has worked on a farm, describes the first time he was shown how to butcher lambs:

> I looked up when I heard a PLOP. The warm hide had fallen to the floor like a wet towel. The lamb now glistened as the gelatinous fatty tissue reflected the bright shop lights.

These examples convince me that the writers knew what they were talking (writing) about; in each case, I'm ready to hear more.

Form

Personal narratives are often structured by chronology: first this happened, then this, which led to that. However, narratives can be told through flashbacks, mixed chronology, and even multiple points of view. Of all the short writing forms, the narrative may have the simplest organizational scheme. This probably accounts for its reputation as an easier form than essays organized by other argumentative and explanatory schemes. But don't be fooled—narrative that seems direct and straightforward may have gone through dozens of drafts to reach final form.

Consider also that new forms and formats can bring new life to narratives. In fact, they are generative, creating new insights even if you only intended to alter the form. In the example mentioned before, Joan began to tell her story of life in the donut shop by looking backward, reflecting in the past tense, "I was a Dunkin' Donuts girl." Later, however, she abandoned that perspective for the present tense created by the journal format: "October 23. I've driven into Durham daily, but no one's hiring." (See Chapter 11 for more of this narrative.) One is not necessarily better than the other; each simply makes both writer and reader experience the event from a different perspective.

In playing with your narrative, in looking for your final point of view, focus, theme, or whatever, consider playing with the form: What would happen if I told this as an exchange of letters? Could the reader experience it differently if it resembled a drama, with lots of re-created dialogue? Could it be tailored for a column in a magazine, such as "My Turn" in *Newsweek*?

READERS AT WORK

When you include descriptions of actual events and places in your story, the accumulation of detail begins to tell your story for you. Let it. In early drafts of narrative writing, authors want to explain to the readers everything that happened, why those things were important, and exactly what the reader should get from reading this. In later drafts I recommend letting your skillful re-creation of details *show* your story to the reader.

Showing works better than summarizing because concrete detail allows readers to *see* your experience and then make their own summary statements. When Kate writes, "He grabs the student around the neck, holding the head tight with the elbow and shoulder," we see the mode of control; had she instead written, "He holds the student so she cannot move," the writer would skip to the net effect of the judo hold, but would deprive us of visualizing it—and in visualizing it, we become more engaged with it and, in turn, provide our own summary or judgment: "she cannot move." Specific detail actually makes a reader work harder in a positive way. When, instead, the writer does all the work, providing the summaries, judgments, and editorials, readers become passive or even withdraw: "I am about to tell you about the hardest job I ever had. . . ." The judgment has been rendered and there's less to do. What you want instead is for readers to enter into the interpretation of your story and actually to help in finding out what it means. The net result is more investment on their part as they enter your story with you and locate themselves within it and figure out what the story you tell means. Recall how Jeff put you in the battery factory or Stephany the egg farm. In these cases, the readers experience the difficulty and make their own judgments. When the reader has done that, you've won.

So What?

While a narrative is based on something that actually happened, keep in mind that the reason you write about it is to portray something about yourself that has some meaning or value and that makes a point. Narratives, just like reports, critical essays, and research papers, must make a point, must have a reason for having been narrated. As a reader, the question I commonly ask when I finish reading is "So what?" What difference has it made that I read this? Why did the author choose to tell me this? As a writer, I try to keep the same question in mind at all times: why am I bothering to tell this particular story and not some other? What do I intend my reader to take away from this reading?

However, making a point in a narrative isn't always easy. Seldom are our lives broken up into neat modules or stories with clear beginnings, middles, or ends. Our tasks as writers will be to fashion convincing lives for our readers, as if such starting and stopping points existed. In that sense, whatever you write as truth will have some element of fabrication about it. Sometimes a narrative will start with a strong directly stated thesis (in the first set of student samples, Frank's "monotony"). However, it is more likely that a narrative lead will imply, but not state, the actual thesis (Sue's "dull throbbing of my lower back" or Jeff's "target waiting to be shocked"). Many narratives make their point through the accumulation of detail, asking the reader to make meaning from a revealed slice of life.

WRITING FROM EXPERIENCE CHECKLIST

1. What story have I told? Is it primarily about me? an event? somebody else?
2. When I finish reading the story and ask "So what?" does my story provide an answer?
3. Have I *shown* rather than *summarized* the action and details of this story? Can you see where it takes place? Can you hear my characters speak?
4. Do I make my readers do some interpretive work? Or do I provide all the judgments and explanations for them?
5. Does my form work? What effect would other forms (journal, letter, essay, drama) have on the story I want to tell?

AUTOBIOGRAPHY

Much of what I have written about personal narratives is also true of autobiography. You usually write in the first-person mode ("I"), from remembered experience, in more or less chronological order. As in personal narrative writing, you remember as best you can, and invent what you need to make it more credible. However, in autobiography you may have an even greater need to be selective and inventive, depending on how far back you attempt to go to make sense of your life.

Scope

What separates autobiography from other narratives is scope and focus. The scope of an autobiography is some substantial portion of your life, and so the advice about taking one small chunk of time and elaborating in great detail is less helpful. With a lifetime of experience—be it 18 years or 48—to account for, it's unlikely that an autobiographer would choose to focus on the smaller moments of his or her life. However, when small moments generate life-changing insight, they hardly classify as "small moments," do they? Keep in mind that no matter how large the scope, it's the particulars that persuade.

Strategies

Two obvious strategies for writing an autobiography present themselves, one inductive, the other deductive. The inductive method would involve the following activities: make a list of what you would call the "important events" in your life: high school graduation, confirmation, reading a particular book, making a new friend, etc. Tinker with the list until it seems a reasonable representation of your life and then start writing—anywhere about any incident—and keep writing to see what themes or patterns emerge that you didn't predict. Take one of these themes or patterns and make that your controlling thesis.

If you want your life story to be strong and meaningful, you will need to discover, fabricate, or invent a controlling idea that shapes the story and somehow gives insight into who you are today and what you stand for: your passion for order or for art, your inability or your readiness to commit, etc. In short, when writing an autobiography, you deliberately select a focus and supporting detail from among the many possibilities to give an external shape and meaning to your life. Remember, your writing will never *be* your life, but only one of many representations, which explains who you are and how you got there.

To write deductively about your life, you reverse the process and begin as if you had something to prove: you start with an idea of a quality or theme that seems to characterize your life: your competitiveness or insecurity; your need to be in control or believe in something; your decision to become a priest or an astronaut; your fascination with words or insects. Your writing then begins to explore this theme, as you deliberately bring to mind all those elements that seem to support this pattern, ignoring incidents that don't help develop your point about yourself. Again, your aim is to fashion a version of your life both believable to your readers and reasonably true to your own conception of things.

Of course, every time I've begun to write about a piece of my life the inductive and deductive have gotten mixed up: I begin to write deductively, believing there is a pattern, and find many elements that are important but don't fit. Then I end up writing inductively to discover what the new pattern may be. But I accept that as one valid way to go about this difficult writing task, perhaps more realistic than either of the one-dimensional modes.

SUGGESTIONS FOR JOURNAL WRITING

1. Make a list of five significant experiences that happened to you during the last year. Write a few sentences about each, noting why it was remarkable, important, or memorable.

2. Make another list of commonplace or ordinary events (non-events?) in your life. Think, for example, of times or places that you remember more for what you expected or thought than for what actually happened. Or think of a routine activity you nor-

mally do, but have not before paid much attention to (mowing the lawn? going to church? closing the family cottage for winter?). Write a paragraph about each and see if, once you focus on it by writing about it, there's perhaps a story to tell.

3. Jot down a page or so about every job you have had in the last four years. What do you remember best about each?

4. Re-create three dialogues (without prefaces) of a page each in which you and somebody else had an interesting or unusual exchange. (When writing dialogue, remember to use quotation marks when people talk and to paragraph each time speakers change.)

5. Select a point in time (birth? 3rd grade? age 12?) and make a list of significant events that you believe have shaped your life since then. Begin to chronicle these in your journal, giving each a fresh page.

6. Do a freewrite in which you explore possible themes in your life. (If you don't know where to start, try out words such as "competitor," or "awkward," or "comic," or "bashful," or "outsider" and see if any fit you.)

SUGGESTIONS FOR ESSAY WRITING

The following assignments should be done in approximately the order suggested; if you take shortcuts you will shut off new and promising possibilities. You can do these assignments in the course of one day or several weeks, allowing some fallow time between drafts. They are best done with other students, in writing response groups of five or so, with each student sharing in turn his or her draft and receiving feedback from the other writers along the way. (For more information on working in small writing groups, see Postscript Two, p. 194.)

1. Select one personal or work experience from among those you listed in your journal and develop a draft paper of about three pages. Let this draft go in any direction it wants to, but try to show the experience by putting us there with you rather than summarizing it.

   When you have finished this initial draft, share it with others and find out their reactions to it. For example, you might ask each respondent to tell you (1) what parts of it were most interesting and (2) where you should provide more information. Using this response as a starting point, begin to play further with your story until you discover additional dimensions. Each time, read your new draft to your writing group and listen to how they react.

2. Write another draft of the same experience, this time finding some excuse to add dialogue to what you portray. (If you aren't happy with the piece so far, start over on the same or a different subject. Do this with caution, however, and never in haste; your best work will most likely occur when you struggle to enter deeply into one experience, in this way writing through and beyond initial frustrations.)

3. Write a third draft limiting the time period to one day, one afternoon, or one hour of the experience. (You might also consider writing this version in the present tense to see how that changes what you say.)

    This close focus should spring loose some specific detail you didn't notice before. Remember, the parts of your experience or job that may be most interesting to others are the parts you now take for granted. It's the crock of pickles at the salad bar and the overheard conversation at the donut shop that tell the story, that convince readers, Yes, the author was there.

4. Write a fourth draft from the perspective of another person connected with the experience, actually assuming his or her voice and describing yourself in the third person ("he" or "she").

    Another's perspective will give you a new way of looking at yourself. "How would your mother remember the same experience? What did your boss think when you did that? How did it appear through the eyes of your best friend?" You really can't just imagine it; you need to actually write it out as if the other person were talking.

5. Write the fifth draft in a new form: If you have been writing a narrative essay, consider a "drama" or "journal" or "letter" format.

    New forms are generative—they actually create new insights. Switching forms often causes you to see things freshly as, for instance, re-created journal entries will make you see the experience from the limited perspective of one day at a time; writing the experience as dialogue will limit the story to what speech can capture, so you might find yourself creating scenes as in a play. (To learn more about these effects, see Chapter 11, "Imaginative Writing.")

6. Look at all of your previous drafts and select the approach that now most interests you (which could combine several of the above) and write a final draft. Ask yourself "So what?" about your

story: Do you want the final focus to be more on "you," "what you did," "an event," or "another person"? In other words, at this point, *what is the story you finally want to tell?* (Append to the final draft, in order, all of the previous drafts written.)

In the end, your finished paper may tell a different story—or be told in a different form or tense—from the one you first imagined. Remember, interesting final-draft writing often results only after other, more exploratory writing has helped it develop.

SUGGESTIONS FOR RESEARCH PROJECTS

1. Write a portion or chapter of your autobiography. Collect from home as much stuff (notes, report cards, baseball cards, old magazines or records, memorabilia, wall posters, journals or diaries, letters, school papers, hobby remnants, etc.) as you or your parents can unearth that says something about your own development as a person. Find a way to weave this story of yourself at one point in time, using some of these documents of personal research to help you.

2. Write a profile of a classmate in which you make him or her come alive. Place everyone's name in a hat, and draw out two at a time. Names drawn together are to interview each other, spend time together, maybe share a meal, visit each other's living quarters, and in general keep talking to and making notes about each other. Write these up after the fashion of "Profiles" printed in *People Magazine*, *The New Yorker*, or your daily paper or as Studs Terkel did when he edited the tape transcripts for *Working* (Random House, 1973). Along the way, share drafts; publish as a classroom profile when all have been completed.

3. Search the library periodical holdings or your own living room for magazines well known for printing interesting nonfiction (e.g., *The New Yorker*, *Rolling Stone*, *Esquire*, *The Atlantic*, *The Village Voice*, *Sports Illustrated*, *Time*, *Newsweek*, *Reader's Digest*, *The New Republic*, *Redbook*). Browse through these magazines and make notes about whatever interests you in the narrative writing you find there. Report—orally or in writing—what you found and how it relates to your own writing.

Chapter 8

WRITING EXPOSITORY ESSAYS

exposition: n. 1. a setting forth of meaning or intent. 2. a precise statement or definition; explication; elucidation. 3. the act of exposing or the condition of being exposed.

Essay writing dominates the liberal arts curriculum, particularly where teachers are liberal and classes small. It's the favorite assignment of instructors in the humanities, a common assignment of instructors in the social sciences, and less common among instructors in the scientific and technical fields. You'll also find essay assignments to be frequent among instructors in business, law, education, and all fields that value critical analysis, logical reasoning, and independent thinking. In short, the essay is a pervasive, powerful, and demanding form of writing to master.

Essays come in many forms and ask for a variety of mental activities, from analysis and synthesis to interpretation and judgment. Often you are required to perform several activities in one paper. To simplify the discussion, I'll use the term *expository* to apply to the many activities that require you to display your reasoning about issues and problems outside of your own experience.

In the last chapter, we talked about writing from personal experience, which is often in the form of personal essays. Many of the criteria for writing them are broadly applicable to essays in general— to convince your reader that what you say is serious, believable, and worth listening to. Like narratives, essays should be organized according to a clear pattern, should contain substantial detail or examples, and should reveal something of the writer's voice. Beyond those rather general statements, it's hard to pin down what, exactly, an essay has to look like or be, because essay writing is essentially a formula-defying activity. In most cases, you write essays to demonstrate *your* intellectual faculties, not to fill in the blanks of someone else's.

In the balance of this chapter and the next we will examine some of the reasons why essays are commonly assigned in high school and college, explore the general expectations common to the form, and describe the mental activities required to write them well.

ESSAY ASSIGNMENTS

Essays provide readers with a great deal of information about their authors. For one thing, they indicate how well writers reason on their own, apart from the tighter constraints of objective testing. For another, essays demonstrate the writers' knowledge and whether it fits some theoretical framework. In addition, essays provide substantial evidence about the writing abilities of their authors. Let's look at each of these points in greater depth.

First, teachers ask you to write essays to see how well you can reason about specific problems. Keep in mind that the word "essay" means (in French, at least) to "try" or "attempt." In general, essays have a speculative or tentative nature about them. Readers don't expect them to contain the last word about a topic. Instead, they expect questions to be addressed with enough intelligence, information, and perspective to make the reader think further about them. When I write an essay, I don't mind that the reader may witness my struggling with a question to which I may not have a clear-cut answer. However, I *do* want my reader to see evidence that the struggle is well reasoned, informed, and literate. In fact, a strong method of ending an essay is to raise further questions that need to be answered at another time, by someone else.

Second, essays should reveal what you know and how well you know it. They demonstrate that you have read, researched, and located certain information and that you understand and can make sense of it. Some documentation may be necessary when you write essays: in many academic cases, you want your reader to see that you are fortifying your own ideas with those of experts in the field. I would include formal references to any sources used in writing an essay. (For simple documentation form, see Chapter 17.) Such extra support or explanation takes a little more time, but assures your reader that you know your business.

Third, essays reveal how well you *write* by revealing your reasoning and knowledge. They demonstrate your ability to write clearly, precisely, correctly, and with grace, style, and wit. In short, in writing essays, *how* you convey your argument and information will be noticed and taken into account.

PURPOSE

Most essay assignments are built around one dominant intellectual task that is more important than the several subordinate tasks you must also perform. For this reason, pay attention to what, exactly, an essay assignment asks you to do. If you need to write an essay in which your primary task is to *explain* how to brew root beer, for example, you may also have to *define* root beer *compared* to other beverages and, at some point, *analyze* and *evaluate* different modes of brewing—all in the service of explaining.

The rest of this chapter will focus on four commonly requested foundational tasks: explanation, definition, comparison, and analysis. The next chapter will examine the somewhat more complex tasks of synthesis, interpretation, and evaluation.

Explanation

> **to explain:** v. to make plain or comprehensible, to make the meaning of something clear; to define or expound; to offer reasons for or a cause of; to justify.

Probably the most common academic writing task is that of explanation, often called "exposition." To explain is to make some concept, event, or process clear to your reader (to expose it). You can do this by researching in textbooks or recopying lecture notes. However, a much better method is to use your own words—perhaps supported by research. In any case, use language appropriate to the discipline and occasion. Your journal is an excellent place to practice finding your own explanation of "the origins of the French Revolution," or "the theme of nature in American literature," or "the Big Bang Theory of creation." Another example is this book itself, which is my attempt to write a series of explanatory essays on writing.

When I teach first-year writing classes, I commonly ask students to join together in small groups to investigate a local issue and, together, write a report to the rest of us explaining its significance. In the following example, a group of six students wrote a collaborative paper investigating the water-treatment plant in the city of Burlington, Vermont. Here, they explain the nature of the pollution that periodically closes the beaches on Lake Champlain:

> The sewage overflow usually takes place after heavy rains.
> The sewage and storm waters are handled by the same pipe, and

the pipe can't handle both the sewage and the rain water. Then the overflow goes to the lake instead of the treatment plant. The real bummer is that the beaches are closed two to three days after.

This example is simple, clear, quite general, and effective for its intended audience. (By the way, the colloquial term *bummer* in the last line is a good indicator of the audience for whom the group is writing—other college students.)

Later in the same essay, the water-treatment group provides a more detailed explanation of the lake pollution:

Vermont has always been a casual, back to nature, "no worries" state. During the last few years the Burlington Sewage Treatment Plant has had problems containing large quantities of effluent that is deposited during and after a rain storm. Its effluent is rich in nitrates, phosphorus and bacteria and the introduction of unnatural levels of substances by the sewage plant is one of the lake's major sources of pollution (Miller 130).

Here, they start off casually, calling Vermont a "no worries state," but quickly get down to business, buttressing their own explanation with a reference (Miller 130) in case the reader wants to check sources. Notice that in both of these examples the writers mix informal with formal language to explain most clearly: In fact, the very best explanations usually use the writer's simplest, most direct, comfortable language. Notice, too, how **explaining** relies on **defining** and **describing** to achieve clarity.

In explanatory essays, your chief goal is to be clear. Clarity is a function of (1) knowing your subject well; (2) organizing your explanation according to some clear scheme (chronology, cause–effect, comparison–contrast); and (3) using simple language, being careful at all times to use the important vocabulary of the discipline.

Definition

to define: v. to state the precise meaning of something; to describe the nature or basic qualities of; to specify distinctly; to serve to distinguish.

Defining is simply a more specialized mode of explaining in which you must be especially precise because defining something means separating it from other similar concepts.

You will seldom be asked only to define something. More commonly, you will be expected to act on your definition. For example, in math you may have to define differential equations and be able to solve problems based on your definition; in psychology you may need to define Freud's theories and apply your definition to a case study; in business you may need to define supply-side economics and make a case for this policy.

At one point in the water-treatment essay, the writers provide us with a technical definition of pollution that is both more inclusive and more precise than their description of Lake Champlain pollution so far:

> In order to talk about pollution, one must define the terms involved. According to the dictionary, "to pollute," means, "to defile, to soil, or to make unclean." This definition is a bit too general for our needs so we incorporate another: "Pollution is the introduction of material or effects at a harmful level" (C. R. Curds and H. A. Hawkes 20).

You will notice that this example presents two external sources for authority—a dictionary and a text on the subject of pollution (Curds and Hawkes' *Ecological Aspects of Used Water Treatment*, 1975). When writing, in the academic world and elsewhere, make your definitions clear and authoritative.

Sometimes, however, it will be necessary to do your own defining, as in the following case, where Susan defines the various strands of contemporary music in order to classify and compare it:

> "Rock Classics" can be loud, raucous, and even noisy at times, but then the band will slow down with gentle ballads. The bands which play this type of music include the following: Led Zeppelin, Jimi Hendrix, Jethro Tull, The Rolling Stones, The Kinks, Neil Young, and even the Beatles.

Susan then provides a definition of several more categories: Heavy Metal, Glitter Rock, and One Hit Wonders. Here, for example, is her definition of Glitter Rock:

> This style of music is characterized by very extravagant, peculiar, and bizarre performers. It is hard to describe, being sometimes screechy, other times quiet. This type of music got its start in the early seventies with performers such as David Bowie, Alice Cooper, Lou Reed, and Frank Zappa.

Susan's task is a difficult one, since music—especially contemporary music—does not succumb easily to verbal definition. However, notice that she uses examples of well-known rock performers to help her clarify what she means. The use of examples typically clarifies and strengthens definitions.

When writing essays that depend heavily on defining something, keep the following principles in mind: (1) in defining a word, use synonyms and not the word itself to make your definition clear (for example, "fish are cold-blooded animals living in water and having backbones, gills, and fins."); (2) illustrate with concrete examples (as Susan did above or as we could do about fish by describing several different species of them); (3) go back to the basics; don't assume your reader knows even the simplest terms; don't be afraid to state what to you is obvious (that, for example, all fish "live in water"); (4) sometimes it's helpful to point out what your definition does not include (the term *fish*, for example, does not normally include whales, lobsters, or scallops).

Comparison

> **to compare:** v. to examine (two or more things, ideas, people, etc.) for the purpose of noting similarities and differences; to consider or describe as similar.

We compare things all the time: this college, city, or state to that; one movie, book, or record to another; and so on. As we compare, we usually also contrast, noting the differences as well as the similarities in our comparison; thus, the act of comparing often includes the act of evaluation as well. In my nonacademic life, I read the magazine *Consumer Reports* regularly to help me choose one product over another; in my academic life, I read *College English* to help me choose one theory or interpretation over another.

Throughout your college studies you will be asked to compare and contrast in order to interpret and evaluate; you will do this as often in business, math, and engineering as in history, philosophy, and literature. However, actual comparative essays are more common in the latter, more interpretive disciplines than in the former, more quantitative ones. For purposes of essay writing, you should be aware of particular *types* of comparison as well as good *methods* for doing it.

Apples and Apples   At a basic level, we compare like things to like things: one apple to another for taste, color, size, etc. We usually compare similar kinds of things to answer questions of worth or suitability: is this the best pen (of several kinds) to write with? Is this the best stereo system (of several brands) for me to buy? Is this the best interpretation (among competing ones) of this poem? In these instances, the elements being compared are similar and do similar things, and thus can be compared point by point.

Apples and Oranges   Most often people use these terms—apples and oranges—to describe a false comparison: you can't ask which fruit tastes better because the two are different. You might prefer an apple to an orange, but it makes no sense to say that one is better than the other.

Analogy   Writers deliberately compare one concept or item to another to make clearer an aspect of one: learning to write may be compared to learning to ride a bike—an analogy that stresses the part of writing that is difficult to teach but, once learned, is difficult to forget. In like manner, it is hard to explain how the human mind works, but making an analogy to the electronic on/off switches of a computer circuit board may help explain it—at least to some people. Writers use analogies to make clear that which is not.

Figurative Language   You are probably familiar with figurative language such as metaphor, simile, and personification from discussions of poetry, fiction, or drama, but here, notice the powerful effect they have on writing that is not fiction, that attempts to show the world as the writer actually sees it, that makes comparisons stick in the mind of the reader. Writers use *metaphor* to compare something abstract to something concrete or something unknown to something known. For example, in the previous chapter Annie Dillard describes a weasel as "a muscled ribbon." Writers achieve similarly vivid results when they use *similes*—a type of metaphor that states the comparison directly by using the words *like* or *as*. Here, for example, is Dillard's whole sentence about the weasel:

> He was ten inches long, thin as a curve, a muscled ribbon, brown as fruitwood, soft-furred, alert.

To make you see this weasel in no uncertain terms—as she saw it—she includes in her definition several literal descriptions ("ten inches," "soft-furred," "alert"), one metaphor ("a muscled ribbon"), and two similes ("thin as a curve," "brown as fruitwood").

    Personification is the metaphorical comparison of inanimate to animate objects—especially to human beings. Notice in the following passage from *The Immense Journey* how Loren Eiseley uses this technique to make us see a landscape as he saw it:

Some lands are flat and grass-covered, and smile so evenly up at the sun that they seem forever youthful, untouched by man or time. Some are torn, ravaged and convulsed like the features of profane old age.

[Vintage Books/Random House, 1957, p. 3]

In this passage, some land is said to "smile," a comparison to a happy human state, and some land is "convulsed like the features of profane old age," a sad human state.

Analysis

to analyze: v. to separate into parts or basic principles in order to determine the nature of the whole; examine methodically.

All academic disciplines teach analysis in one form or another. When you analyze something, you must find a logic that holds it together and use that logic to take it apart. Essentially, analysis requires that you identify what parts make up a whole and that you then look closely at what parts make up each part. Depending on your discipline, of course, you may be asked to analyze a story, an argument, a social group, the circulation system, or the universe—all require a similar mental operation.

A simple example of an analytic task could be found in something as common as a table. Depending on your purpose, a table might be analyzed according to structure (legs, braces, top); type (drop leaf, trestle, end); shape (round, oval, square); purpose (dining, coffee, work); or materials (wood, metal, plastic). Each component can be broken down further: the category of wood into oak, cherry, pine, walnut, etc.

For an example of analysis, look again at the water-treatment essay collaboratively composed for my writing class. The group handed out a survey to citizens of Burlington to find out how much they knew about pollution on Lake Champlain. In order to report the results, they had to collect, tabulate, and **analyze** (make sense of) the responses. Here is how they reported the results of their analysis:

85% of the people realized there is a serious sewage problem in Burlington. 65% realized Burlington's drinking water comes from Lake Champlain. 70% knew that the beaches closed because of the sewage problem. 40% blamed the sewage problem on the city, 40% blamed it on the treatment plant, 10% did not think there was a problem, and 10% did not answer. Only 30% of the people bought water because of the problem. . . . A surprising 65% said it is worth the estimated $52 million to fix the problem.

This survey further proves that most of the people in Burlington are aware of the serious nature of the sewage problem in Lake Champlain. However, they were not fully aware of the toxic materials being dumped in the water.

Notice that the analysis here depends upon a simple methodical tabulation of quantifiable survey answers and the consequent drawing of conclusions based on the counting. (Notice also that the writer starts sentences with numbers; convention prefers that numbers at the beginning of sentences be written out; thus eighty-five percent rather than 85%.)

Another kind of analysis occurs when people study texts to see what they mean. To **analyze** a poem, story, or article, for example, may require that you take apart the language or structure to locate small bits of meaning. For example, John, a student in my first-year writing class, analyzed a sports story on the Boston Celtics written by Associated Press reporter David O'Hara. To demonstrate that O'Hara is wrong in predicting a successful Celtics season, he focuses on a passage quoting Larry Bird:

> "We're going to be good this year," Bird said. "We're playing a lot of different players, and we're doing a lot of different things. It reminds me of the 1986 team."
>
> O'Hara quotes Bird, which gives the fans hope and sells tickets. Bird doesn't mention that one of the reasons the Celtics are playing a lot of players is because of . . . "age." In this case age is not all that good either. "Experience" comes with age, but so does "fatigue."

Each of the tasks described here has a distinct expository purpose: to make certain information or ideas clear. After reading an explanation, definition, or analysis of something—or comparing it to something else—readers are often in a position to do something else with the information—for instance, make a new synthesis from it or develop an interpretation of it or evaluate it.

In the next chapter we will look at **synthesis**, **interpretation**, and **evaluation**—some fairly complex essay writing tasks that commonly build upon the kinds of information developed in expository forms. As I said at the beginning of this chapter, most essays involve a number of reasoning tasks, so this division of essay writing is to some extent arbitrary, useful especially for making two short chapters on essays rather than one very long one.

SUGGESTIONS FOR JOURNAL WRITING

1. Your experience as an essayist has been a long one, probably dating back to third or fourth grade. In this respect, you already know a lot about writing essays. For this journal entry, reflect back on your successes and/or failures as a writer of essays. What seems to determine the quality of your essays? What techniques work for you? What don't? Can you determine why?

2. Write out each of the operational words used in this chapter (e.g., *explanation*, *definition*, *comparison*) and then see if you can define each in your own words.

3. Make a list of possible topics about which you might write an analytic essay in this writing class. (Or, if you need to write an essay for another course, make a list of possible topics for that course.) Then jot down, next to each, the dominant and subordinate mental operations you will perform to write a good essay. (For example, if I were to write about the effect of lamprey eels on the trout in Lake Champlain, I'd probably have to *describe* the problem, *explain* why it exists, *define* terms I think you may not know.)

SUGGESTIONS FOR ESSAY WRITING

A NECESSARY PREFACE: Authors usually write essays to explore subjects and share their explorations with readers. Such essays are published in popular periodicals, professional journals, and as collections in their own right. Essayists such as Ellen Goodman, Russell Baker, Mike Royko, and Erma Bombeck write regular columns for daily papers about whatever current issues cross their minds. Essayists such as Lewis Thomas and Stephen Jay Gould write to explore ideas particularly associated with natural science. Meanwhile essayists such as William Buckley and William Raspberry—in the tradition of James Madison and Thomas Paine—write primarily about politics. In each case, the writers choose to write about what they know and care about.

In contrast, when students are asked to write essays for school writing assignments, these same conditions of choice, interest, curiosity, and a desire to share, are seldom present. Instead, school essays often become required work connected to specific avenues of study, about which students may or may not have any interest: explain the Magna Carta for history; define the mole concept for chemistry; compare the ideas of John Stuart Mill to Jeremy Bentham for political science; analyze Picasso's *Guernica* for art history; build (synthesize) a solar-powered vehicle for mechanical engineering; interpret a Shakespeare sonnet for English; evaluate a particular marketing strategy for business.

I leave it to you to select the particular topic to explore. Essay writing can be truly pleasurable and can lead to profound learning and new insight, but you need to be interested in and curious about your topic for this to be so. The following suggestions should help you get started, but, in truth, your best essay topics will come from your own concerns and curiosity.

1. Think of two or three possible majors that you might pursue in college. Define, explain, and analyze each. Then compare one to another according to criteria you select: what you are already good at; what you want to be good at; how you want to earn a living; and what you want from life. Write this essay to share with your classmates to persuade them that you have made the right decision for yourself—or that you are at least on the right track. Write in the first person, including as much hard evidence as you can to support your reasoning.

2. Do the previous assignment collaboratively, as a member of a writing group, selecting the same intended major and jointly drafting an essay to which you each contribute. Share your group essay with another group, they theirs with you, and act as editorial review boards for one another. Plan to publish the results in a collection to leave for next year's students to read and respond to. (Of course, your instructor will need to be the agent of transmittal if you choose this option.)

3. Select any topic that you are interested in—sports, politics, art, automobiles, and so on—and write an essay in which you deliberately look at it from several perspectives. Be aware that you are writing in the essay tradition and keep your voice speculative and exploratory. Conclude in a way that suggests further exploration of this subject is in order, that makes clear that your essay is not meant to be the final word.

SUGGESTIONS FOR RESEARCH PROJECTS

1. **INDIVIDUAL:** If you're curious about essays as a form of writing, research the origin and history of essay writing. Where did it begin? What cultural conditions made it a useful form? Who were the masters of it in past centuries? Do essays serve a useful purpose in contemporary American culture?

2. **COLLABORATIVE:** This can be done with any size group—the more the merrier: agree on a local institution (pizza parlor, drug store, teen center, library—the smaller the better). Each of you write individually about this place, focusing on something small and concrete (conversations overheard in a booth, action at the checkout counter, etc.); share your drafts, noting the different approaches each essayist took; finally, select editors and bind the results together as a book to share with those who own or work in this place.

Chapter 9

WRITING INTERPRETIVE ESSAYS

This chapter is best looked at as an extension of the last chapter on exposition. In many ways it is artificial to separate *interpretation* from *exposition*—or for that matter to claim there is any writing that is not, in some sense, interpretive. However, the focus here is on writing that is deliberately created to make a particular meaning from a book, event, experience, idea, or information—with the full realization that other meanings will be made from the same material. In other words, I would argue (itself an act of interpretation) that the difference between interpretation and exposition is the writer's awareness that his or her assertions are matters of argument, subject to debate, and admittedly persuasive rather than conclusive. Certain areas of study such as literature, philosophy, and religion seem to lend themselves more obviously to interpretive writing than others, say mathematics, chemistry, and physics. This seems so in part because literary, philosophical, and religious questions seldom have agreed-upon answers while the more scientific disciplines do—at least at elementary levels of understanding. But at the frontiers of every scientific discipline, things are still up for grabs—that is, open to interpretation. And as soon as one asks social or political questions of scientific knowledge, one is again involved in matters of interpretation (more on this issue directly).

In this chapter we will look at some of the kinds of essay writing you are likely to do in college, where you are frequently asked to *synthesize, interpret,* and *evaluate.* We'll conclude the chapter by looking at the nature of essay examinations and some strategies for successfully writing them.

Synthesis

to synthesize: v. to combine parts to form a new whole; arranging and combining elements or pieces to make a pattern or structure not there before.

All academic disciplines teach synthesis. To perform this operation, you put ideas or elements or parts together—sometimes things that don't seem to belong together—to form a new whole. Synthesizing may involve different operations, depending on the discipline, but in all it means putting elements together to form a new whole. In chemistry, when you combine chemicals, you produce a chemical synthesis—a new *synthetic* material may result. In history, a synthesis may involve combining one historian's theory of historical development with that of another, and so on.

The ability to synthesize is prized in both the academic and the nonacademic world, because it implies that you know not only how to take things apart, but also how to put them back together, which is the work of builders, engineers, scientists, doctors, lawyers, artists, literary critics, and teachers, among others. It might be argued, however, that the ability to synthesize is a survival skill necessary to all of us in an increasingly complex world.

An example from my discipline would be the following question, commonly asked in essay examinations: "You have read three different American writers—Emerson, Thoreau, and Whitman. Identify and explain one theme common to all three." You may need to begin by *analyzing* each work, making notes or an outline of the major points in Emerson's essays, Thoreau's *Walden*, and Whitman's *Leaves of Grass*. You find that Emerson looked to the natural world for ethical lessons, that Thoreau made a spiritual symbol of Walden Pond, and that Whitman revered the smallest as well as the greatest creature in the universe. You've now got evidence for the theme of "nature" that connects all three.

In the following student example, notice how the writers of the waste-treatment essay referred to in the last chapter arrive at a synthesis at the end of their paper by making recommendations based on their research discoveries:

> The first and most important thing to do is reduce the amount of your buying. If you don't absolutely need the product then don't buy it. You don't need a chemistry degree from U.V.M. to reduce hazardous chemicals in your home. You can do the following:
>
> 1) When you're buying a product make sure that if it's hazardous there are directions on how to dispose of it. If you buy something you're responsible for disposing of it.

2) Don't buy it unless you really need it.

3) Don't buy more than you need. Getting rid of the extra can be annoying.

4) Use the safest and simplest substances that you can find.

5) Recycle whatever you can: Used motor oil, paint thinners, battery acid (and batteries), automatic transmission fluid, diesel fluid, fuel oil, gasoline, kerosene, motor oil, and even dry cleaning solvents can be refined and used again just like aluminum cans. (See Appendix C.) If you're not sure what to do see the "Household Hazardous Waste Chart." It was adapted from the Water Pollution Control Federation pamphlet, 1987.

In this case the **synthesis** becomes, in the end, an **argument** for water conservation. Finally, the writers also attempt to **persuade** their readers to act as a result of reading this essay.

As you have probably figured out by now, people don't set out to write pieces called "synthesis essays." Most often they have been explaining or analyzing something and find the need to make suggestions or draw inferences based on that work. In the following example, John concludes his critique of the Boston Celtic story. Having analyzed this particular story's shortcomings, he **synthesizes** to create a lesson of sorts about sports writing:

Maybe sports stories should raise questions that make you think. Sports Illustrated seems to offer both sides to many stories, as they offered two sides to Boston Celtic Len Bias's cocaine over-dose. Granted, magazines are different than newspapers, but newspapers can make the effort. The audience for newspapers is much larger, and its impact is more widespread. It may help someone develop into a "thinker" instead of a "follower" just by reading the newspaper.

Interpretation

to interpret: v. to explain the meaning of; to expound the significance of; to represent or render the meaning of.

Interpretation is another specific form of explanation especially useful in the academic world. Interpretation implies that there may be more than one explanation with merit; your job is to point out why a particular meaning is the best possible or the most probable. As I suggested at the beginning of this chapter, interpretation is especially important in so-called humanistic disciplines such as history, literature, philosophy, where almost all concepts are a matter of one interpretation versus another: What was the chief historical cause of the war in Vietnam? Was it ideologic, economic, or geographic? Kant believed one thing, Hegel another: With which philosophy do you most agree? What did poet Robert Frost mean in the poem "Stopping by Woods on a Snowy Evening"? These questions should be regarded as matters of interpretation rather than as having right or wrong answers.

Don't think, however, that interpretation applies only to the arts and humanities. When political scientists conduct an opinion survey, different political scientists will interpret the results to mean different things. When the economic indicators point to inflation or recession, liberal economists will explain things one way, conservative economists another—a matter of interpretation. Some biologists believe dinosaurs became extinct because the climate changed gradually, others because it changed rapidly when a large meteor collided with the earth; physicists differ in their explanations of the origin of the universe as chemists still argue about proper definitions of the atom—more matters of interpretation. In each of these examples, experts make a *guess*—called an hypothesis—that such or such is the case, but cannot prove, beyond a doubt, that they are correct.

In the following example, Mary **interprets** the meaning of a painting, *Inner Energies*, by artist Tracy Leavitt, in this way:

> The artist is trying to point out that technology is running away from us.

Jason, however, interprets the same painting this way:

> Thus this portrait is the expression of the woman's drive to identify with man's accomplishments.

While Ron suggests:

> With this idea Leavitt suggests that we are not following God as we should be.

In other words, **interpreting** a work, an event, an idea may lead different writers to different conclusions. Just be sure that your interpretive statement is supported by data, analysis, and/or expert opinion. The best interpretations are those that convince others to believe you.

Another kind of more personal—and more general—**interpretation** occurs at the end of Steve's critique of Robert Frost's poem,

"The Road Not Taken," when he sums up the poem's meaning as a lesson in life:

> There comes a time in life when people have to make a decision, and people often wonder what it would be like had they made the other choice. That is what "The Road Not Taken" is about. If you take life too seriously, you are going to miss it. You have to take it one step at a time. If something does not go your way, you must learn not to dwell on it.

In this instance, Steve says the poem means this to "you." Yet I actually see his statement as a very personal one. (Were he to work further on this interpretation, I'd suggest he change the pronouns from "you" to "I" and "me.")

The most common interpretive acts in college may center around poetry and fiction. In most cases, your teacher will want you to be more precise, to stick closer to the text than Steve has above. An especially important part of interpreting is demonstrating where you got this or that idea—which often means bringing into your text a passage from the text you are interpreting. In the following example, Katherine quotes a line from the poem, "Elegy for Jane," by Theodore Roethke:

> The poet leans over her grave and speaks his last words to her, "I with no rights in this matter/Neither father nor lover." He can do nothing now, and feels remorse that he never expressed to her his love. Love, Roethke seems to argue, must be shared when it happens or it will be lost forever.

Here, of course, we see just how much an act of **interpretation** depends on careful **analysis** in the first place.

Look at a final example of interpretive writing as William investigates the meaning in Charlotte Perkins Gillman's short story, "The Yellow Wallpaper":

> We begin to question [the narrator's] emotional state when she envisions the wallpaper lady creeping, by daylight, through the estate grounds. At night, the narrator struggles to set her imaginary friend free. At the climax of the narrator's breakdown, she falls to the level of a child's mentality. We cannot help but pity her when she begins to gnaw at the wooden bedframe out of frustration. She becomes a child in her own world—at last, secure. The story ends with her claiming, "Here I can creep smoothly on the

floor, and my shoulder just fits in that long smooch around the wall, so I cannot lose my way.''

John was ludicrous in claiming that his wife was suffering from only ''temporary depression.'' She was a full-time mother, wife, and writer. She was also a victim of a full-time mental illness which required attention if ever to escape from it. Since the woman never received the necessary help, she eventually disintegrated to the level of a child.

In this example we see the documentation of the problem in the first paragraph, then the writer's conclusion, based on it, in the essay's last paragraph. A good job of interpretation.

When you write interpretively, keep in mind that (1) your interpretation is one of several that may have merit; (2) you must support assertions with evidence—direct quotations are especially useful for interpreting the meaning of texts; (3) you must separate fact from opinion; (4) qualifying words (*perhaps, maybe, might*) show that you are still open to other possibilities; and (5) you must define, explain, analyze, and evaluate carefully as you work out your interpretation.

Evaluation

> **to evaluate:** v. to ascertain or fix the value or worth of; to examine or judge carefully.

To evaluate implies judgment, finding the merits and faults of something. Like the other operations described here, evaluation should be based on some analysis or interpretation already performed in the same essay. Evaluation is crucial, at some level or other, to every academic discipline: you evaluate one theory against another; one set of facts against another; one piece of art or music against another; or you evaluate against criteria.

In other words, you can evaluate in several ways, just as your teachers do when they must arrive at student grades: In one case evaluation is against an absolute standard—each student in a class could theoretically get an ''A'' or an ''F'' this way. In another case, you evaluate by comparison/contrast—the best students get high marks, and the weakest fail, regardless of absolute standards. Some evaluation is carefully quantitative—points for everything are totaled; other evaluation is highly subjective—impressions determine all.

Evaluation, like synthesis, necessarily draws on many of the other activities described here: analysis, definition, explanation, etc. In writing evaluations of colleagues, schools, proposals, book manuscripts, students, I usually lead off with the most objective statements first, both pro and con, and work up to an overall evaluation that makes a recommendation in one direction or another. This procedure allows those reading my evaluations to see the criteria on which I made my recommendation and answers in advance many possible questions—a good suggestion for student writers.

It should be obvious by now that categories described here overlap: John's **synthesis** about sports writing is also an act of **evaluation** as he renders a judgment about good and not so good sports writing. William's **interpretation** of "The Yellow Wallpaper" is also a tacit **evaluation** about the profundity of the story he has read. Let's look at other occasions where deliberate acts of evaluation are called for.

Here are two concluding paragraphs from essays my students wrote reviewing a collection of essays entitled *Models for Writers* by Eschholz and Rosa. Kyle writes:

> If you pick up this book and read just one story you will see for yourself why this collection of essays is so good. It may be used for pleasure or as a text. This not only makes for enjoyable reading, but also provides a learning experience for the reader. By combining these two types of reading in one book, the editors produced a book that can be enjoyed by all.

Kyle's statement comes at the end of an essay where he has looked at specific contents of the book in some detail. Nevertheless, he takes greater liberties than I'd recommend with his closing generalization that "the editors produced a book that can be enjoyed by all."

Obviously enough, few experiences can be enjoyed by all. A useful suggestion for college writers: Avoid ending with a meaningless little flourish. Quit a line early instead.

Betsy writes a summary evaluation of the same book this way:

> I feel the editors have put this book together well by picking authors and essays that will appeal to college students. Who would ever think that Steve Martin would have an essay in an English book as a model of good writing? I think by having such authors the student will be more willing to turn to this book for help. I find this book has many enjoyable essays and would recommend it to anyone who has to write papers.

I prefer Betsy's conclusion because she works in at least one concrete reference (Steve Martin) and also raises an amusing question. There's a liveliness here. She too, however, tacks on an unlikely last line, recommending the anthology "to anyone who has to write papers."

One of my first-year writers, Amanda, wrote an account of her experiences picking potatoes on her father's farm in Scotland, a job that used to be done by sixty workers, but is currently done by a gigantic mechanical harvester needing only four people to run it. Amanda's conclusion to her experience is evaluative in a moving way:

> This year the potato harvester is still working, the same women on board, with the same bored expressions on their faces. Soon this job will probably not need anyone to work or help the machinery. Labour is an expence farmers cannot afford. There are no tattie holidays anymore, no extra pocket money for the small children of the district. Change, technology, development is what they say it is, I say that it is a loss of a valuable experience in hard work, and a loss of good times.

In this example, part of the flavor and the strength comes from Amanda's informal conversational tone, which convinces us that a real human being is speaking humanely.

Evaluation is often in order when you find these direction words: *compare, contrast, choose, evaluate, rank, measure, judge, justify, agree, disagree, argue, prove, make a case for*. In writing an evaluative essay, it's a good idea to (1) establish what exactly you are evaluating, (2) describe it thoroughly, (3) assess its strengths and its weaknesses, and (4) be fair in the language of your final recommendation, avoiding obviously emotional or biased terms as much as possible.

VOICE

When you write interpretive essays, use a comfortable voice, not so relaxed as in a journal, not so objective as in a laboratory report— unless you have a good reason to diverge from this middle point. For more formal situations, avoid contractions, first-person pronouns, colloquial diction, split infinitives, and the like—but don't use language you are uncomfortable with or try through pretentious words to impress. For informal situations, use conversational language, keeping in mind that readers look especially closely at your organizational scheme and use of evidence in analytic essays. If your essay is solid in these respects, you have some license with your voice.

FORMAT

In essays, as in most writing, form best follows function. For me, this means paying particular attention to the task asked for—being analytical when asked to analyze, being judgmental when asked to evaluate, being clear and thorough when asked to explain. Some teachers will not term what they ask for an "essay" but may ask you instead simply to write a *paper* on this book or that subject. In these situations, it's a good idea to remember that you are being asked to display what you know, how you reason, and how well you write.

GENERAL QUESTIONS TO ASK YOURSELF

While essays vary greatly in what they attempt to do, the following list of questions may help you assess how well your particular essay is achieving its purpose. These are good questions to have friends or classmates answer about your essay—and you about theirs:

1. What is my essay trying to accomplish? (Is this purpose stated clearly in the essay? If so, where?)
2. How is my essay organized? (Would subheadings help the reader follow my organizational structure?)
3. Are my assertions supported by fact or opinion? (How can the reader tell? Have I documented my facts?)
4. Is my voice consistent with my subject and intention? (How could I describe my tone and style? Are they consistent throughout?)
5. Does my introduction introduce? (Can I think of other ways to start this piece?)
6. Does my conclusion conclude? (Can I think of alternate ways to end this piece?)

WRITING ESSAY EXAMINATIONS

This discussion wouldn't be complete without a note about writing essays as in-class examinations. Everything in the discussion of essays holds true for essay examinations, except that you have little or no time to revise what you write. Actually, in performance, essay exams more closely approximate highly focused freewriting than out-of-class essay writing. Nevertheless, there are a few things you might keep in mind when preparing to write these high-pressure essays:

1. Use writing to help you study for the exams in the first place; it's much better actually to *write* out practice essay answers

in your journal than just to *think* the answers. Your at-home practice writing will tell you quickly where you lack the concrete resources to answer the question well, and the phrases you use in practice will come forth readily in your actual exam setting.

2. Do some quick brainstorming on scratch paper before committing yourself to the actual exam answer. This advice is difficult to follow, but it will pay dividends, especially in organizing your essay answer.

3. Try to write a thesis statement at the beginning of your answer and spend the rest of the time supporting it, saving your best support for last.

4. If you can't write a thesis statement initially because you need to write for a while to find it, then work as methodically as possible on the blocks of support most likely to lead to it, and state your thesis clearly at the end in a separate paragraph that looks deliberately placed.

5. Use paragraphs as your unit of construction: indent for each new point because that increases your teacher's chances of seeing individually each point you make.

6. Keep in mind that the strongest points of emphasis in an essay are at the beginning and the end; when you are able, make your strongest points at these places.

7. Remember that essays are assigned to let the teacher see your range of reasoning and knowledge. For the latter, you need lots of correct facts; but for the former, it's a good idea to show your ability to raise questions and ponder possibilities in addition to giving limited and set answers.

SUGGESTIONS FOR JOURNAL WRITING

1. Reflect for a few minutes, in writing, about your experience writing essay examinations. Have you been fairly successful at it or not? What factors seem to determine how well you respond to an exam?

2. Write out each of the operational words used in this chapter (e.g., *synthesis, interpretation, evaluation*) and then write your own definitions in your own words.

3. Make a list of possible topics about which you might write an interpretive essay in this writing class. (Or, if you need to write an essay for another course, make a list of possible topics for that course.) Then jot down, next to each, the dominant and subordinate mental operations you will perform to write a good essay.

SUGGESTIONS FOR ESSAY WRITING

1. Select a text from this or another course you are currently taking and locate within it something that interests or puzzles you, or that you disagree with. Write an interpretive or evaluative essay about the text using your specific interest as a point of departure. Plan to end this essay with still another question that your readers themselves might pursue or puzzle over. In other words, end with an admission that more needs to be looked at; the writer herself or himself still has uncertainties.

2. Attend a play, concert, lecture, or other public event and write an interpretive or evaluative essay about your experience. Contact your local or school newspaper and see if they'll publish it.

3. Do assignment (1) collaboratively, as a member of a writing group, selecting the same text or event, and jointly draft an essay to which you each contribute. Share your group essay with another group, they theirs with you, and act as editorial review boards for each other. Plan to publish the results in a collection to leave for next year's students to read and respond to. (Of course, your instructor will need to be the agent of transmittal if you choose this option.)

SUGGESTIONS FOR RESEARCH PROJECTS

1. **INDIVIDUAL:** Select any topic about which you are curious or have an opinion (informed or otherwise). Visit the library or a local museum and locate information which both supports and rejects your own ideas, or arguments about this topic. Take good notes and write an essay that synthesizes, interprets, or evaluates the information you found there. (You might reflect on whether this additional information in any way changed your mind or if it simply made you find more evidence to back up your initial opinion; write this reflection in your journal.)

2. **COLLABORATIVE:** Agree to disagree. In a small group, identify an issue, idea, or place about which you each have only a little information. Divide yourselves into research teams, go get some information, write it up, and share it with the group. Then, each of you take a deliberately different approach or slant on the topic and write a series of essays meant to be read in a colloquium, together, to air all sides of the issue. In class, present a series of such colloquia to entertain each other. Publish the results.

Chapter 10

SET PIECES

> It was really the student newspaper . . . that developed me into a writer: 2 A.M. at the printers, a ten inch hole on page one, Mr. Barta yelling that he would go home in an hour whether we were finished or not, someone on the phone calling in the facts, and me writing those ten inches, nearly as fast as I could type—ah, the virtues of formulaic writing.
>
> Richard M. Coe, in *Writers on Writing*, ed. Tom Waldrep.
> New York: Random House, 1985

Some writing tasks are more routine than others. Sometimes I know exactly what I want to say, making discovery drafts unnecessary— when, for example, I write out the directions for making hot Mexican salsa (which I know by heart) or record the minutes for a faculty meeting. Other times, the purpose is clear, the audience familiar, and no great decisions hang in the balance—when, for example, I write a thank-you note to my mother or a memo to colleagues scheduling a meeting. Although accuracy and clarity are important, it simply would not be good use of my time to spend too long getting these communications "just right."

People who work in various professions, businesses, or agencies do a substantial amount of writing that might be called routine, including proposals and reports, directions and instructions, summaries and abstracts, and letters and memos. Examples of routine academic writing might include short informational papers, abstracts, summaries, book reviews, literature surveys, lab reports—all assignments where matters of form are fixed, and the writer's business is to report information clearly but not necessarily with grace, style, wit, or imagination. Essay exams and quizzes fall into this category also, because such writing usually focuses on *what* you write rather than *how* you write it. Assignments such as these don't *exclude* creative and innovative approaches, but in many cases the form is set, the expectations are clear, and your time is limited.

Because we all must do this kind of writing from time to time—sometimes because the task demands it, sometimes because we've planned our time poorly—it's good to know some shortcuts. I've chosen to call these kinds of writing "set pieces"—writing best generated from established guidelines or "sets" that let you concentrate on content rather than style or structure.

In this chapter we'll look at the foundations of set pieces. Such writing is meant to communicate information clearly, directly, and succinctly to readers already familiar with the form in which you are writing.

TOPIC SENTENCES

The building blocks of routine writing are topic sentences and thesis statements. These are meant to be clear, direct statements of purpose that govern paragraphs in the first instance and entire compositions in the second. Make sure you know what topic sentences and thesis statements are, how to use them, and when your readers will expect to find them in your writing.

Topic sentences introduce the theme, direction, or substance of paragraphs. When you write with them, they should help you shape and control the direction of your thought; when you read them, they should help you to follow where the author is going. If you want your readers to follow your writing with little chance of misinterpretation, uncertainty, or wandering, provide them with a clear topic sentence for each paragraph (like the one that begins this paragraph). What you lose in surprise you will gain in predictability. In this kind of writing that's a good trade, because a reader who can predict where you are going next will understand you most clearly if you do, in fact, get there. This won't always result in the liveliest or most imaginative writing, but it's the closest thing to a guarantee for clarity that I can think of, and clarity is highly prized in academic and technical writing.

Another way to look at topic sentences is to see them as generalizations that the rest of the paragraph must support. A friend of mine even goes so far as to provide a formula, teaching students how to construct paragraphs that most faithfully adhere to the topic sentence concept. He teaches students to write paragraphs the following way:

write a topic sentence; write a second sentence that expands the first; write a third that qualifies the second; add a fourth that provides an example relating to the previous sentences; and conclude with a transition to your next paragraph.

I present this formula partly in jest, because few serious writers would follow so mechanical a procedure in putting thought together. However, if you have had trouble figuring out exactly what paragraphs are supposed to do, practice constructing a few paragraphs this way, and you'll learn the idea of coherence as a governing principle. Actually, there's nothing quick and dirty about topic sentences at all. When they develop from prior paragraphs and anticipate further development, they become the cornerstones of much well-organized writing both in academia and elsewhere. Learn why they work and how to support them, and you'll seldom be faulted for clarity.

THESIS STATEMENTS

Thesis statements introduce the theme of the whole piece of writing. If papers are written in answer to questions—implied or explicit—it is the thesis that announces the direction that the answer will take. A thesis stated up front in a paper makes the writer's intentions clear and anticipates the reader's question of "So what?" My thesis for this chapter is direct and succinct: "Some writing tasks are more routine than others." The rest of the chapter is my attempt to elaborate on and support that assertion. However, if you look at my first chapter, you will find the thesis near the *end* of the first paragraph: "This book is written to introduce you to some of the general expectations and practices typical of college communities. . . ." In both cases I make clear early on what these respective chapters will be about, giving you the option of reading more in them.

For academic writing, the direct approach is the safest. When in doubt, lead with your thesis. Lead with the best articulation of it that you can muster, and then move on, keeping that assertion always in mind, elaborating on it, substantiating it, qualifying it, but always referring back, directly or indirectly, to that opening statement of purpose holding the piece together.

If you were reading a pile of history papers having something to do with the Battle of Gettysburg, which of the following theses would most invite you to continue?

1. The Battle of Gettysburg was one of the most interesting battles of the Civil War.
2. Geography played an important role in the Battle of Gettysburg.

3. The North got to the high ground first, and the North won the Battle of Gettysburg.

In my judgment, the first sentence is a weak thesis: to call something "interesting" may be polite, but it's not in itself interesting. The second sentence, however, announces one of the specifically interesting aspects of the battle, geography, and so invites the reader to learn more about that—it makes a decent, though unexciting, thesis. The third sentence appeals to me even more: this writer suggests that he or she knows exactly where the essay is going right from the start and promises to do so in a lively prose style.

If there is one general set guideline to follow in academic writing, one you would do well to internalize, it's to write your academic papers so that on the final draft a clear thesis statement is both apparent and supported—a guideline that presumes, of course, that you have information and ideas about which to frame theses.

SUMMARIES

A summary reduces a long text to a shorter one by condensing the main ideas and skipping the details. For example an "executive summary" may be a one- or two-page document that condenses a much longer piece of information into a form readable in a few minutes. A "book report" (as opposed to a "book review") summarizes the main plot, theme, and characters of a book. The following are a few guidelines for writing summaries.

1. Keep your primary objective in mind: to reproduce faithfully the main ideas of a longer document, skipping the details.
2. Be accurate and brief: condense paragraphs to sentences, sentences to phrases, and skip sections that you judge redundant or unnecessary. (Don't, however, reduce the piece to an outline that only you can understand.)
3. Write in your own clearest style. A summary is about information: it is more important to be clear than to be true to the style of the original document.
4. Follow the organizational pattern of the original: if the original has subheadings or numbered points, use them as guides for writing your condensation.
5. Maintain the tone of the original as best you can. If the source is witty, be witty; if the source is formal, be formal (or wittily formal or formally witty).

ABSTRACTS

An abstract is a condensed summary. It summarizes the important points of a given text. But whereas a summary of an article may be one or two pages long, an abstract will be less than one page long. An abstract of this chapter might go something like this:

> Set pieces of writing follow predictable formats in order to be done quickly and efficiently. Set pieces include (1) topic sentences, (2) thesis statements, (3) question/answer formats, (4) summaries, (5) abstracts, (6) five-paragraph themes, (7) reports, and (8) reviews.

Abstracts may be routine, but they're not easy. They are difficult because you must *thoroughly* understand the piece you are abstracting and because you have so little freedom to use your own language. To write them, follow the general advice for writing summaries, only more rigorously. Of course, the one necessary preparation for writing abstracts is to be thoroughly familiar with the piece you are abstracting. You might consider writing a paragraph-by-paragraph topical outline first, including just the topic sentence of each paragraph. Then see if you can cluster these under more condensed headings, and so on. (It helps if the piece itself is set and follows a predictable pattern, including thesis statement, topic sentences, and the like.)

REPORTS

A report describes an event or tells a story about something. You may have written a book report (a description of what happened in the book) or a laboratory report (the story of what happened during an experiment). If you are assigned to write reports in a particular class, your instructor will specify what kind of report and give you guidelines for what it should look like.

Reports require information to be conveyed to an audience clearly, directly, and succinctly: a progress report on a project or research paper, a report on a lecture or film that you attended, or a report on available resources to proceed with a project. You may often relate such information in any order that makes sense to you (and, you hope, to your audience). However, in some disciplines the forms for reporting information may be highly specific, as in the sciences and social sciences, where reports generally follow a predictable form.

Research Reports

I found the following format recommended in both biology and psychology for reporting the results of experiments; forms similar to it will be used in other social science and "hard" science areas as well:

1. Title: a literal description of the topic of your report.
2. Abstract: a summary in 250 words or less of the why, how, and what of your report.
3. Introduction: a statement of your hypothesis and a review of the relevant literature.
4. Methods and materials: information that would allow another experimenter to replicate your work.
5. Results: charts, tables, and figures accompanied by a prose narrative to explain what happened.
6. Discussion: a review of your results, a comparison to other studies, and a discussion of implications.
7. References: a list of all sources actually cited in your report, using appropriate documentation format (see Chapter 17).
8. Appendices: work pertinent to your report, but not essential to understanding it.

In the event that you are asked to write a technical report, I would consult one of the many report-writing handbooks used in technical writing or business writing courses.

Journalistic Reports

We might also look briefly at reports as journalists do, as "reporting." Journalists train themselves to ask a set of questions, the 5 W's, about every event on which they report: Who? What? Where? When? Why? (and sometimes How?). The advantage of remembering a set of routine questions is obvious: writing reports for daily papers requires fast writing with little time for revision. Reporters actually call these reports "stories" and commonly write them in one draft, composing in their heads, while driving back from the scene of the accident, fire, speech, or whatever they have been assigned to write about that day. (At least one reporter has told me that he sometimes begins composing the story on the way *to* the event.)

For rapid composing, nothing beats a set of second-nature questions that help sort out new information by putting it into preset categories: Who is this story about? What is the issue here? Where did it occur? When—what time of day? Why did it happen—what caused the situation to develop as it did? And how did it happen—how did the events unfold? These questions are variations of those a lab scientist or a novelist might ask, as they attempt to provide a framework for talking about the world and what happens in it—be that piece of the world one's laboratory, one's news beat, or one's *Oz* or *Wonderland*.

On those occasions when you are asked to report something that happened in a meeting, concert, or public event, using the journalists' questions will quickly organize your information.

REVIEWS

The act of reviewing really has two useful academic definitions. The first implies that you simply go over something a second time in the interest of thoroughness or reconsideration. In many academic disciplines, especially the social sciences, it will be expected that formal papers begin with "a review of the literature," which implies an organized summary-level listing of the previous research relevant to your topic. While you are expected to highlight the main points of the most useful studies, you are not expected to critique them. Literature reviews are to demonstrate that you have done enough reading to be well informed on your topic; they establish your credibility as a student of the field and provide your reader with initial evidence of your viewpoint and direction.

A review of this chapter would highlight the forms of writing being explained and point out that each is accompanied by some advice for performing those tasks well. A review in this first sense would neither praise nor criticize the merits of the chapter's explanation or advice.

Critical Reviews

The second meaning of the word *review* implies criticism or judgment, as in critical review. Such a critique is essentially an assessment of something, usually pointing out both strengths and weaknesses, such as we have come to expect in book or movie reviews. Furthermore, we often expect some kind of a recommendation about whether to read the book or see the film. Another name for a critical review would be "critique." Note that to do such a critical review essay well would usually require skillful incorporation of the other intellectual tasks we talked about in the last two chapters: exposition, definition, comparison, analysis, synthesis, interpretation, and evaluation.

Book Reviews

Book reviews are a likely academic assignment in a variety of subjects. In writing a review, there are some things to keep in mind:

1. Provide all necessary factual information about the subject being reviewed (for example, book title, author, date, publisher, price). Do this early in your review, in your first paragraph or as an inset before your first paragraph.
2. Provide background information, if you can, about the writer and his or her previously published books.
3. Follow a clear organizational logic (comparison/contrast, general to specific, etc.).
4. Support all assertions and generalizations with illustrative, specific examples from the book being reviewed.
5. Evaluate fairly, keeping your obvious personal biases in the background.
6. Write to the knowledge and ability of your particular audience. Modify your language according to the degree of familiarity your audience has with the subject (reviews imply that you are doing a service for someone).

There are no fixed rules about length or format when writing reviews. However, if you're in doubt, here are some safe guidelines to follow if no others are provided: allocate approximately one-fifth of your review to factual information and background; one-fifth to explaining the book's subject matter; two-fifths to an evaluation of the strengths and weaknesses of the book; and one-fifth to a recommendation of the overall worth of the book.

Better than an arbitrary formula would be to look at published book reviews. The best place to find examples of critical reviews for books (and movies, plays, records, and products) would be in popular periodicals such as *The New York Times Book Review*, *The Atlantic*, *Harper's*, *Esquire*, *Rolling Stone*, *Time*, *Newsweek*, and *Consumer Reports*. Refer also to the professional journals in your field of study—in my case I'd look at reviews of English books, specifically in *College English* and *Modern Fiction Studies*, and more generally in *The Chronicle of Higher Education*.

FIVE-PARAGRAPH THEMES

A theme is an expansion or elaboration on a given topic, akin to an essay. However, a five-paragraph theme is more an exercise than an essay. Five-paragraph themes are structures that enable student writers to say something coherent and organized in two to three typed pages. They are built around thesis statements and topic sentences; they depend on careful transitions; and they demand clear introductions and conclusions—all in five paragraphs. They are worth learning because the skills needed to write them are transferable to a variety of brief (in time or space) academic composing projects, such as in-class impromptu essays, short argument papers, and essay examinations.

Five-paragraph themes are written this way: (1) lead with a thesis statement in your opening paragraph that makes a general case for some topic; (2) follow with three paragraphs that support or debate the issue introduced in the first paragraph; (3) make sure that each paragraph begins with a topic sentence and ends with a transition to the next paragraph; and (4) conclude by moving once again to generalizations about the subject you have just talked about, sometimes suggesting implications, other times raising questions for further consideration.

If you learn to write such brief two- to three-page papers, with that movement from general to specific to general, you will learn how to write a variety of other forms along the way: short position papers, executive summaries, opinion papers, book reviews, research notes, and essays both informal and analytical. This is also the basic form desired on placement tests, college admissions essays, proficiency examinations, and the like. Of course, it seldom matters that you have *five* paragraphs—three, four, or seven may be written in precisely the same manner. What matters is that you meet your readers' expectations that you will introduce a topic, explain and illustrate it, and say something conclusive in a few minutes of reading time. It is not, however, writing meant directly for the world outside of school. Its highly formulaic nature makes it of limited usefulness to real-world writers.

ANSWERING QUESTIONS

One final note about set pieces. It sometimes helps me to keep in mind that virtually every piece of writing answers a question. In that sense, I can turn even complex writing assignments into more simple tasks: analyzing a poem answers a question about how the poem works or what it means; narrating a summer work experience answers a question about what you did last summer; describing a light bulb answers a question about what a light bulb looks like and does. It's helpful to keep this in mind when writing almost any kind of assignment that doesn't already have an internal structure: the question/answer format gives you one, as you can open with the question both in your title and in your lead paragraph, an opening as useful to you as to an audience who wants to find out what you have to say.

If, for example, you are asked to write a paper on a current issue such as an equal rights amendment, a quick way to get a handle on the assignment is to jot down possible questions—the answers to which would essentially constitute your paper: why do we need such an amendment? What problems would such an amendment address? To whom would it apply? What changes would it make?

Ultimately, a set piece is any form, such as personal or business letters, that you know well enough to write comfortably. However, some very "set" forms, such as memos and business letters, are *not* set for you if you're not familiar with them. The next chapter looks at some writing that is less familiar by design, a form we'll call "imaginative writing."

SUGGESTIONS FOR JOURNAL WRITING

1. What kinds of set pieces do you most commonly write now? What kinds have you written in the past? In your own words, explain the procedure for writing one of these forms.

2. Is there a particular kind of set piece that you would like to learn? How do you now go about writing it? What about writing it gives you the most difficulty?

3. Composition books such as this may be considered set pieces in some ways, trying to give certain advice to writers on all the necessary points of writing the author can think of. Examine this book as a set piece by comparing it to other composition books you have had in the past. What about it strikes you as different? What's the same?

SUGGESTIONS FOR ESSAY WRITING

1. Select a paper you have already written for this or another course and write a summary or an abstract of it. Exchange with another student and help make each other's papers even tighter, shorter, and more precise. Conclude with a note about difficulty doing this type of writing.

2. Write a review of this or another book you are currently using for this course. As a class, compare your results with the brief suggestions you find in this book. Would you modify or expand any of them? Would you add any new ones?

SUGGESTIONS FOR RESEARCH PROJECTS

1. **INDIVIDUAL:** Look in the library for examples of a set piece you would like to master (e.g., book reviews or lab reports). Study these pieces and see if you can arrive at any guidelines that seem to govern their creation. Write out these guidelines and then write one piece of your own that follows them.

2. **COLLABORATIVE:** Meet with a group of students who are equally concerned with learning a particular set form (as above) and agree to divide up research responsibilities for learning more about it: (a) some of you visit the library and locate examples; (b) someone interview an expert or two on the form; and (c) someone collect from faculty members examples of whatever guidelines they use. Share this information with each other and develop your own set of guidelines, perhaps composing a paper to illustrate them in practice.

Chapter 11

IMAGINATIVE WRITING

> Unlike the arts of painting and music, literature, as far as schools and universities were concerned, was not something that students DO, but always something that other people HAVE DONE.
>
> James Britton, *Prospect and Retrospect*, ed. G. Pradl. Boynton/Cook, 1982

Sometimes, the writing assignments you get in school beg to be played with. You know when these come along by some combination of the assignment itself—wide open or imaginative and the personality of the instructor—easy-going or unorthodox in some way. When these circumstances combine—and if you're inclined—take some risks and have some fun.

Other times instructors will challenge you directly with a provocative assignment that tests your imaginative wits. Suddenly, you have to write something for which there are few rules and absolutely no formulas: to write a technical report from a fictitious business; to solve an imagined case problem; to role-play two authors talking to each other; to imitate the style of Hemingway or Faulkner; to write a poem, play, or short story; to invent a new ending to a story; to create a utopian community.

For either writing task—the one you frame for yourself or the one assigned—keep in mind that no matter how much you play with form, style, or theme, teachers remain interested in the strength of your ideas and how well you support them. However, if you can present these ideas in a lively and interesting fashion, you increase your chances of being listened to and heard. The trick is to have fun and, at the same time, to demonstrate, illustrate, describe, explain, defend, or embed in your piece ideas as strong and well supported as you would in a more conventional paper. In this chapter we will look at some techniques for doing this.

PLAYING WITH THEME

To write a playful paper on any subject, you've got to get the theme right. To play with theme implies that you know that theme backward and forward and that your playful rendering will make that point perfectly clear. Think of the circus juggler or the water skier who clowns around while performing astounding feats of balance and coordination—how obviously skilled they must be to make it look so simple. When you write something unorthodox in college, you're in the same predicament: you've got to make it seem unusual and orthodox—or silly and serious—at the same time. This is tricky. Theme in a novel may involve "nature" or "appearance versus reality"; theme in history may involve "great men" or "class struggle"; theme in philosophy or political science may involved "idealism versus materialism"; and so on. In any case, theme will encompass the ideas that a given book, unit, or course is all about.

If, for example, you were assigned to recreate a fictitious dialogue between Plato and Aristotle to show their philosophical differences, you would be sure that Plato represented the "Platonic" ideas just as Aristotle represented the "Aristotelian." Naturally. More difficult, however, might be your decision to write an alternate ending for a Virginia Woolf novel or to recreate a "lost sonnet" of Elizabeth Barrett Browning; in either case, while you would have to get the form and voice just right, you would also have to be thematically consistent with the beliefs of each writer and the context within which she existed.

The matter of theme would also be relevant in a playful assignment in one of your business classes, where you would have to ground your approach in carefully articulated theory and documentable fact. For example, to role-play a dissatisfied customer suing an automobile dealer over a recently purchased "lemon" would require that you reveal a thorough knowledge of car defects, the terms of automobile warranties, and your state's lemon law. In like manner, to write a convincing scenario of a manned spaceship landing on the planet Mars for a physics course would require an accurate projection of the physics of the imagined situation, combined with demonstrated knowledge about the Martian environment.

To play with theme in your imaginative writing, keep the following ideas in mind:

1. Know thoroughly the authentic themes of the writer, writers, or situation from which you are deliberately stretching, modifying, or taking off.
2. Be consistent in your theme play; if you exaggerate at the beginning, remember that in subsequent sections of your piece.
3. If you play with theme, can you also play with voice and format?

PLAYING WITH VOICE

The term *voice* is used here to describe the essential character of the writer as revealed in written language. (For more information about voice, see Chapter 18.) Voice is a matter of both content and style: you find content in the sentences that reveal something about the writer's beliefs and values; you find style in the writer's choice of words, level of formality, and the rhythm of his or her sentences. There is, of course, a voice of sorts in all writing (and speaking), but the writer sometimes goes to great lengths to conceal it, as in scientific and technical writing. To play with voice suggests that you know your own writing voice(s) and that you can imitate others' voices as well.

To assume a voice other than your own in a business or technical report may mean concealing the obvious features of one's voice in favor of a certain kind of neutral-value language best described as voiceless. To adopt the authentic language of such writing would involve studying it enough to replicate its features: formal sentences, passive grammatical constructions, no contractions or first-person pronouns, but plenty of documentation—even if imagined.

To assume a fictive voice in your literature class may mean quite the opposite—an exaggerated re-creation of a very idiosyncratic author's voice. For example, suppose you were assigned to write an imagined dialogue between J. D. Salinger and Walt Whitman. The trick would be to write, in each author's characteristic tone and style, new and convincing sentences, perhaps merging real with imagined quotations. For Salinger you might want those talky sixteen-year-old adolescent phrases; for Whitman his expansive, often effusive, free verse.

In writing this last paper, your ability to recreate the studied voices of these modern American writers would be more crucial than for re-creating a dialogue between Plato and Aristotle for a philosophy class. Why? Literature study is concerned with a writer's voice in a way that most other subjects—philosophy and political science, for example—are not. In addition, the voices of Salinger and Whitman are unique in the literary world, while many other voices—especially those translated from ancient Greek—have fewer identifying stylistic features.

To play with voice in any assignment, keep in mind the following points:

1. Learn the identifiable features of the style you plan to imitate by studying the specific language features thoroughly.
2. Be consistent in your imitation; check for uncharacteristic lapses into your own particular style.
3. Try to match "theme" and "format" to your voice so that your imaginative piece has a consistent wholeness about it.

PLAYING WITH FORM

The specific form each imaginative piece of writing takes will vary according to the task to be completed. Some forms, such as memos, are easy to imitate because the form is both simple and predictable; other forms, such as poetry, are difficult because they so often are complex and unpredictable. If you have a traditional form to imitate or depart from, study it carefully so that your writing does just that. To imitate a technical report with appropriate sections, subheadings, and documentation is one thing; to imitate a poem with correspondingly careful attention to meter, rhythm, and rhyme is clearly another. The easiest formats for you to play with are those with which you are most familiar.

Form is one of the first things noticed by readers. You expect a certain kind of language when you encounter a title page, abstract, and table of contents attached to a document. You expect something else if the piece begins with a salutation ("Dear Henry"); something else if it's accompanied by an emotive headline; and something else if it's indented a certain way on a page and is fourteen lines long. As a writer, you can build on reader expectations and design your writing to take advantage of the relative strengths of these different forms. As you must guess, there are no rights or wrongs; rather, forms that do *this* well rather than that.

To play with the form of a piece of writing, here are some things to keep in mind:

1. Know well the form you plan to imitate and know exactly what its particular virtues are and what kind of information it carries most effectively.
2. Be consistent in your construction of the form; if you use subheadings in one part, use the same kind in subsequent parts.
3. Integrate "theme" and "voice" into your imagined form in a suitable manner.

JOAN'S FICTIONAL DIARY

> **fiction:** n. 1. an imaginative creation or a pretense that does not represent actuality but has been invented. 2. a lie. 3. a literary work whose content is produced by the imagination and is not necessarily based on fact.

In this chapter I want to share with you one piece of imaginative writing that combines fact with fiction. In one recent first-year English class, I assigned students to write personal narratives about some facet of their lives. (See Chapter 7.) Joan, a twenty-year-old student, chose to write about her experience as a waitress at a Dunkin' Donuts coffee shop. But before she created an imaginary form, she wrote a more conventional draft of a personal essay:

> I was a Dunkin' Donuts girl. Just another face behind a pink hat and a grease-stained uniform. The job could have been degrading if I ever let it get under my skin. To get the job I had to be able to count out a dollar's worth of change and read.

After this lively start, however, Joan wrote the piece as if it were a letter home to her mom:

> Dear Mom,
> If you could see me now . . . I'm a Dunkin' Donuts girl. I was so tired of job hunting day after day that when I found work here I couldn't say "no." I was kind of surprised that I was hired right off the street, without any questions about my work experience or character, but I'm not complaining. It will put food on the table and gas in the car.

Here Joan is writing a simulated letter home. She went on to fashion a series of letters to show her involvement over time, and then she decided she'd have to create some from her mother as well.

Narrative writing usually gains by close focus and concrete detail. Joan wanted to focus close enough to show us her daily life in the donut shop from a behind-the-counter perspective. ("Each customer got only one napkin because they cost 3½ cents apiece.") But the real story Joan wanted to tell involved her progressive disillusionment with her work over several months (her actual theme), so her problem became one of form: which form could both contain the nitty-gritty everyday detail and yet cover a span of three months?

Joan kept experimenting with the shape of her story until she found one she was pleased with—a daily diary. The diary form, while fictive (Joan hadn't really kept a diary during those months), solved her problem nicely. In it she could convincingly portray time passing, keep her piece rich in detail, and avoid sweeping, overly easy generalizations. Her diary started with this entry:

Oct. 23 I've driven into Durham everyday looking for work, but no one's hiring. Today for the 25th time I asked "Who would I talk to about applying for job here?" And for the 25th time I was told "I'm sorry, but we're not hiring right now. But if you'd care to fill out an application anyway . . ." It takes every bit of strength I've got to walk out the door with my head up . . .

Joan is taking personal experience writing an imaginative step further. She's making up a form, inventing dates, re-creating dialogue, reimagining details to carry the truth she wants to tell—which is essentially what writers really do. And she's finding room for this in her freshman composition class. Her diary continues after she finds a job at Dunkin' Donuts:

Oct. 29 My work outfit is a khaki dress, garnished with an orange apron and a pink jockey hat. The clothes are old and worn, grease-stained and mended by hand with many colors of thread.

I tried the uniform on, adding a pair of old white nurse's shoes from the depth of my closet, and went to admire myself in the mirror. My reflection took me by surprise—I looked just like every Dunkin' Donuts girl I've ever seen! The only part of me left was my face.

Tomorrow is my first day. Already, I'm nervous, wondering if I'll do a good job. . . .

Joan's solution worked well, as it allowed her to describe with purposeful immediacy yet keep the reader suspended in the present, living through the fall workdays with Joan herself quite close. We can *see* her as a Dunkin' Donuts girl because she shows us real facts and colors; but had she forgotten the details of the uniform, she could have either invented them or, more likely, made a visit to another Dunkin' Donuts to recapture what she'd forgotten. In the following entry, Joan imagines a dimly remembered piece of conversation to add credibility to her narrative:

Nov. 23 I almost quit my job today, and I'm not sure why I didn't. Mr. Stacy brought me face to face with his temper, and it lives up to its reputation. He went wild, yelling and swearing at me because I only had two pots of coffee made and he thought there should be more. He shouted, "Customers equal money, see? And we can't have customers without coffee, can we? You have to watch these things!"

Sometimes a narrative will start with a strong thesis stated right up front. For example, Joan might have written: "Dear Reader, let me tell you about how I became disillusioned with my job as a fast-food worker and how I decided to attend college instead." But she didn't choose to tell her story that way, preferring to let the reader see the more subtle process of disillusionment as it actually occurred over a period of several months. The last entry she writes for us begins this way:

Dec. 7 I wonder how much longer I'll be at Dunkin' Donuts? There's no room here to move up or get a raise. I can't imagine doing this job for another ten or fifteen years, like some of these people I work with. The turnover is high and the names on the schedule change every week. . . . Starting to look at "Help Wanted" ads again—or did I ever stop?

Joan's finished diary totaled seven fictional diary entries that together comprised her five-page narrative paper. There were, of course, many other more conventional ways she might have told the same tale—as a narrative focusing on highlights, as a series of flashbacks from her present college life, as part of a larger essay on work, etc. For Joan, writing the narrative assignment through this fictive method brought it to life in a way both she as writer and I as reader thoroughly enjoyed.

WRITING FOR FUN

Role-Playing

In role-playing you assume the perspective of someone else and attempt to write as consistently as possible from that perspective, seeing the situation as that person is constrained to see it. For example, you could describe life in the pre–Civil War South from the point of view of slave Frederic Douglass or from the point of view of his white master or mistress. A good format for such an assignment might be an exchange of letters, a dramatic scenario, or an imaginary interview on a late-night talk show. In other words, in addition to re-creating each character's voice accurately, I would hold my piece together in a format in which these characters would actually speak their opinions—imagined yet authentic.

Imagined Dialogue

This would be a particular version of role-playing. Here, the format is to some extent prescribed by the problem. In what circumstances would these two characters be likely to meet and talk? For example, an imaginary conversation between Edgar Allan Poe and Stephen King might be set in a bar, a haunted house, or a cornfield, depending on whose turf you wished to use.

Imitation

Your task here is to write in the style of the work you are studying. You might attempt to mimic the prose or poetry of a favorite writer, or re-create the political speech of a president or the patter of a game show hostess. Of course, it helps to imitate a stylistic extremist, someone whose writing is distinctive. In any case, to do this effectively, you need a thorough knowledge of his or her style, which you might gain by practicing in your journal before you tackle it on the assignment itself.

Re-creation

Your task here is to invent new endings for classic works, such as a new ending for Shakespeare's *Hamlet*, or to devise a missing chapter from Thoreau's *Walden*. I would first determine what thematic difference your change would make; then recreate the act/scene/line format of the original play, paying close attention to details. If you do this carefully, you'll teach your audience something about the writer whose work you are re-creating and experience the work in a new way yourself.

Hypothetical Situations

Common assignments in disciplines such as business and engineering might ask that you solve this or that creative problem given certain conditions. For example, you are a vice president in charge of developing new uses for the bricks your company manufactures; your task is to write a report explaining some of these new options to the company board of directors and recommending a marketing plan. You must stick close to the style and format of a real company report: I would be sure to use a formal title page, subheadings, and graphs and charts.

Parody

A particular form involving any of these ideas is to write a parody of something serious. Parody is, of course, a well-respected genre in its own right; I think of Jonathan Swift here and his classic essay "A Modest Proposal," in which he suggests relieving the famine in Ireland by eating the children. A parody is a possible response to any serious content, especially if the writer wishes to make a point at the expense of some of that content. The same rule applies: know well the object of your parody.

Something Else

The flaw in all of these suggestions is that they are actually assigned often enough so that conventions have developed for doing them well. More gutsy still would be your own invention of a voice, a form, or a theme not anticipated by either your instructor or this chapter. In response to an open assignment in a contemporary literature class, a friend of mine once gave his instructor two loaves of bread, one white and bought in a store, the other whole wheat and baked at home. He attached a brief note stating that American culture was at a crossroads and would have to choose one direction or the other, each symbolized by one of the loaves. My friend survived well because he knew his instructor and his instructor knew him—knew that he was capable of first-rate conventional responses as well.

In this chapter it is best not to have given too many examples or suggestions: the fun you have should be your own.

SUGGESTIONS FOR JOURNAL WRITING

1. Describe any past experience in which you have responded to a school assignment by taking a risk. What happened? Was your teacher pleased with the result? Were you? What did this experience teach you?

2. When you were reading the passages about imitation, re-creation, and parody in this chapter, what author or work came first to mind? What element of this author or work would you choose to imitate, re-create, or parody?

3. Add to this chapter one new idea for an imaginative assignment for your classmates to try.

SUGGESTIONS FOR ESSAY WRITING

1. Select one conventional assignment for a course you are now taking and write it according to some of the ideas in this chapter. (If you intend to hand it in for a different course, clear it with that instructor first.)

2. Select one paper already written for this (or another) course and rewrite it in an alternate form, keeping intact the essential ideas of the original piece.

3. Write an imaginative re-creation of some portion of this or another book you are using for this course.

4. Write guidelines for taking risks in one of your classes to another student in that class, in order to help the other write such a piece successfully.

SUGGESTIONS FOR RESEARCH

1. **INDIVIDUAL:** Research the literature in your intended major and see if you can discover if there is, in fact, any tradition of writing that you might describe as playful, unconventional, or fictive. (I'm thinking here of projects such as that of B. F. Skinner, a noted behavioral psychologist, who wrote the science fiction novel *Walden Two* to convey his ideas to a popular audience.)

2. **COLLABORATIVE:** Interview selected professors at your institution about the major premises of this chapter—that responsible

risk-taking and imaginative writing are worthwhile writing activities. Write up, share, and compile the results of these interviews; create a useful student guidebook to such writing at your institution.

Chapter 12

COMPOSING: HOW TO

9/5   I start by writing down anything that comes to mind. I write the
      paper as one big mess, kind of like freewriting. Then I rewrite it
      into sentences. I keep rewriting it until it finally takes some form.

                                                                    [Brad]

9/5   If I have the time before I begin to write (which I usually don't) I
      make an outline so I have something to follow. An outline kind of
      gives me a guide to fall back on in case I get stuck.

                                                                [Jennifer]

9/5   Then I start in the middle because it's easier than trying to figure
      out where to start. The ending is easy because all you do is repeat
      what you just said. After the middle and the end, I try to write the
      beginning.

                                                                     [Pat]

Everybody writes a little differently from everybody else. Each of the
writers quoted here has his or her own special way of beginning to
write. If it works, it's the best way for that writer. At the same time, if
you're never quite sure how to begin, or haven't yet found your own
best way, the following strategies might help. This chapter looks at
three parts of what might be called "the process of composing":
drafting, revising, and editing.

DRAFTING

When I draft a piece of writing, I try to establish direction, the main form of the argument or story, and some sense of beginning, middle, and end. When I revise, I pay attention to getting the whole paper just right; organizing the material, supporting my arguments, getting down essentially what I want to say. When I edit, I pay attention to the smaller details of writing, to getting the particular sentences and words just right, working on matters of style, precision, diction, and correct documentation. First, some ideas about getting started:

Start Writing to Start Writing

Write your way to motivation, knowledge, and thesis. No matter what your subject, use language to find out more about it. What do you already know about it? What do you believe? Why do you care? (Or why don't you?) Where could you find more information? And so on. This writing will help in two ways. First, it will cause you to think connected thoughts about the subject for a sustained period of time, a far more powerful, positive, and predictable process than staring at the ceiling or falling asleep worrying about it. Second, it will create a written record in which to conduct further digs, records to prompt your memory and help you continue a thought. (I keep such records in my journal, others keep them on index cards. It doesn't matter where; what matters is keeping them somewhere.)

Make an Outline and Promise Yourself Not to Stick to It

In other words, outlines are helpful as starters and prompters, but they are harmful if they prevent further growth or new directions in your draft. I don't always use outlines when I write, especially on short projects (fewer than ten pages), trusting instead that I can hold my focus by a combination of private incubation and constant rereading of the text before me. When I do outline on shorter papers, what proves most helpful is often the very process of generating the outline in the first place; if it's a good outline I quickly internalize its main features and go from there. On longer projects, I am more likely to outline at some point in my writing, but not necessarily before I start. I seldom stick religiously to the formal method of outlining taught me in seventh grade, but like Jennifer (above), I find an outline useful to fall back on when I get stuck. When I do make a detailed outline, I find it easier to see coordinate and subordinate relationships in my project, although I almost always discover these after I've been writing a while and not in my initial outline. The alternation of writing/

outlining/writing/outlining often works well, because both the outlining and the writing are acts of discovery for me.

Plan to Throw Your First Page Away

Once you actually begin to compose a draft on lined pads of paper or,
as I do now, on a computer monitor, don't lock yourself into keeping
the first words you produce. In fact, I find it quite helpful deliberately to view each first paragraph or page as a throwaway. The
absolutely worst part of writing for me is starting, staring at a blank
page or monitor. If I can just get some words down, the task looks
started, and I relax a bit. I've learned that once I start, my words
come a lot easier, and I shift from the slow first gear into progressively higher gears as my thoughts begin to accelerate. When this
happens, my writing not only comes more easily, it's better writing.
In this sense, I agree with Brad (above), who started out fast to create
an initial mess to refine later. (Freewrites, as discussed in Chapter 3,
are helpful here.)

Learn to Write with a Word Processor

Any brand of computer using any word-processing program is helpful. Computers have done to typewriters what typewriters did to
fountain pens—made them nearly obsolete. (Actually, fountain pens
are making a comeback for personal writing, but for academic writing you will always want typed copy.) Word processors make writing
somewhat easier, primarily by allowing you to write words elec-
tronically on a screen before you print them out in ink on paper. The
advantage is that you can move language around as you see fit, until it
is just right. Because I rewrite virtually everything, excepting notes
and journal entries, word processors allow my writing to be more
careful, organized, and precise than on lined pads of paper. Having
my text on a disk also allows me to use an automatic computer
spelling-check program to help me proofread. If you use a word
processor, try to get in the habit of composing first drafts right on the
screen; that will save you a lot of time in the long run and help you to
see your first draft as primarily an experimental one. (See Postscript
One, p. 189.)

REVISING

Plan to Rewrite Everything

More than once, if you can. Good writing is rewriting, reseeing your
first words and determining whether or not they do the job you want

them to do. The more drafts you are able to manage, the better your final piece is likely to be. If you've got a week to do a given assignment, start something in writing the first night and see where it goes; plan to reread and return to it as often as time allows. If you compose in longhand, write in pencil, double space, on only one side of lined paper—this lets you add and subtract from your initial draft with a minimum of recopying and allows you to cut out and move around whole portions of your text.

Attend First to the Larger Problems

Thesis, organization, and support should be re-thought first; edit later to solve sentence-level problems. It's simply more efficient to spend time getting your whole paper in order first, before you turn your attention to the somewhat smaller matters of style—getting just the right turn of phrase, deleting unnecessary words, changing repetitions, and the like. It's more efficient because you don't want to perfect sentences and paragraphs that you would prefer to delete in a later revision. The last stage of editing is proofreading, in which you check for spelling, punctuation, and typing errors.

Write Your Introduction Last

Here I agree with Pat (above), who plans to start in the middle. Of course, if you are able to introduce your piece before you write it, do so. But if you have been outlining and reoutlining, freewriting and journal writing, and finding new ideas and combinations of ideas as you've been going along, it's unlikely that any introduction written first will still do the job. I often try to write introductions first, to point me in a certain direction, but by the time I'm finished, I always need to write a new one.

Seek a Response to Your Writing

Once you have written a passable draft, one you feel is on the right track but far from finished, ask a classmate or friend to read and respond to it. When I do this, I usually specify the kind of feedback that would be most helpful. Does my argument hold up throughout the whole paper? Do I use too many examples? Which ones should I cut? Does my conclusion make sense? Sometimes, when I am quite pleased with my draft, I simply ask a friend to proofread it for me, not wanting at that point to be told about holes in my argument or redundancy in my text.

Write with Titles and Subtitles

Good titles help you view your writing as a whole, and good titles catch readers' attention, pique their curiosity, and describe what your writing is all about. Subtitles (subordinate titles, or subheadings) are words or phrases that stand for a set of ideas or a section of a paper; write them in the margins and let them help you structure your paper for both you and the reader. Subtitles do two things at once: they serve as categorizers for concepts, and they operate as transitions from one concept to the next. I try to do this as early as I can, but I find both the main title and the smaller subsections most clearly when I revise. (You see that I use many subtitles in this book. Are they helpful to you?)

EDITING

After you have your piece of writing pretty much complete in terms of ideas, arrangement, evidence, and thesis, you will want to turn your attention to smaller matters of word choice, sentence rhythm, precision, economy, and correctness. Most writers call this work *editing*, fine tuning a paper to get it just right.

Many times you will write sentences that are adequate and correct mechanically, but that don't convey your ideas with force, economy, precision, and grace. Other times, your first draft will need to be reshaped because you are writing to a particular audience, and you need to change certain words to shift your emphasis slightly in one direction or another in order best to meet that audience. To conclude this chapter, consider some of the more common editing problems and possible techniques for solving them.

Too Many Words

If you take more words than necessary to convey an idea, you run the risk of allowing your reader's mind to wander—unless those extra words do something else, such as create a mood or tone that somehow complements your message. Professor Richard Lanham calls this extra verbal fat "lard," and suggests that good writing will have little of it. When you write such clogged-up sentences, as I commonly do on first drafts, you can usually spot the lard when you read it over a second or third time. I read aloud to myself and listen for the places where the language sounds thick. (In the previous sentence, the first version read like this: "I read out loud to myself and am able to hear when a sentence is not economical." I didn't like the rhythm or precision and so recast it.)

Sometimes sentences are clear and correct but filled with words that don't pull their own weight. In such instances, the simplest edit may be crossing out such words to speed the flow of thought. In the following sentences, I have put brackets around the words that I would delete:

> I found [that] this book [was] [very] easy [for me] to read.

The following words are often clues that lard can be found: "that," "which," "very," and prepositions such as "of," "for," and "from." The original sentence had 12 words; the rewrite has 7—a lard factor of 42 percent.

Sometimes a clogged-up sentence can be recast quite simply by identifying the nature of the clog. In the following case, too many prepositional phrases slow down the reader:

> The success of a company can be attributed to the market analysis of the executives of the company.

To rewrite this sentence I would go after the three "of" constructions and see if I couldn't put my meaning another way, like this:

> The company's success can be attributed to its executives' market analysis.

In this rewrite, I simply recast two modifying phrases ("of a company" and "of the executives") into possessives and dropped the third ("of the company"), believing it unnecessary. Such a sentence could be modified many other ways, of course, depending on the actual context of the paragraph in which it occurs. The original sentence had 18 words, the rewrite has 11—a lard factor of about 40 percent.

Writers commonly think their way through a piece as they write it; the result is often sentences stretched overly long as the thoughts tumble out one after another in an order that may be logical but is seldom economical. Here's an example of this problem from a first-draft paper:

> The focus of this paper is to study how knowledge is structured in the discipline of philosophy. Dr. Miller's class, "Introduction to Philosophy," is the object to be studied and reflected upon.

The clues that this could use rewriting? We see the usual clues: two "ofs" and three "is's." But we also see the repetition of key words ("study" and "philosophy") in back-to-back sentences, which makes me think the two sentences may have exactly the same subject and perhaps could be combined. Here is a possible rewrite:

> This paper will examine how knowledge is structured in Professor Miller's "Introduction to Philosophy" class.

This fairly simple revision reduced this expression from 32 words to 15—a lard factor of 64 percent.

Indirection

Sometimes verbs are the problem. Look at the following pairs of sentences, and see if you can locate the lard:

1. They made a decision to buy carrots.
2. They decided to buy carrots.

In the second sentence, the single active verb "decided" does more and better work than the three-word phrase "made a decision." When you find such constructions, go for the one word that does something, that kicks, shoots, runs, jumps, talks, thinks, challenges, or decides.

In the following pair of sentences, which sounds more to the point?

1. It is a strong introduction that catches the reader's eye.
2. Strong introductions catch the reader's eye.

In this case, the writer simply takes too long when she says "It is a strong introduction that catches." Looking for the word that conveys the action (catch) and moving it closer to the subject (introductions) makes the statement both briefer and more forceful.

Here is another pair to consider:

1. The tomatoes in the garden were planted by me.
2. I planted tomatoes in the garden.

In the second sentence, "*I* planted" the tomatoes. Many of us use the verb "to be" too much; it's difficult to avoid, but other verbs can often provide more vitality in your sentences.

Pretension

Writers often work too hard for profound effects and sometimes end up with unintended effects. The following sentence strikes me that way:

> Oftentimes the great sea of society does not totally corrupt the human heart; sometimes it just makes the natural man writhe in disillusionment. . . .

The writer wants to sound literary by using metaphor, but she's trying too hard for effect, which here resulted in a mixed metaphor ("sea," "heart"). She'd do better putting it simply and directly. Here is a possibility:

> Society does not so much corrupt people as disillusion them.

Unclear Ideas

At times a sentence seems so awkwardly written that the meaning becomes unclear. Your reader then must make a judgment call about whether you are being sloppy with language or you don't know what you are talking about—or both. Here are two examples from a group of book reviews written by students. The following sentence is from a first draft written about Studs Terkel's collection of interviews, *The American Dream*:

> Apparently interested in the American Dream or under the assumption that the reading world would somehow be taken in by it, [Studs Terkel] transferred the recordings into black and white in the exact language they were spoken in.

I have two problems with this sentence: first, I think the writer is being critical of the author when he writes "apparently," "under the assumption," and "taken in"; but the rest of the review doesn't support this, so I wonder why the sarcasm is unexplained. Second, the indirection of the last clause puzzles me: Why does the writer use "black and white" if he simply means writing? I would counsel directly literal terms unless the writer has good reason to use a metaphor. Careful editing would result in clearer meaning.

In the following sentence, written about a chapter in another Studs Terkel book, *Working*, I'm hard pressed to understand what the writer is trying to say.

Mike, a steelworker, shows this where he felt that when he worked on a building, that somewhere it should show that he had some part in building it.

The only way to rewrite this fairly is to go outside what is given here, back to the text, and see what "Mike, a steelworker, shows." I think the problem is first-draft awkwardness, but the lack of clarity could be a lack of comprehension, in which case we are talking more work on the writer's part than mere editing. When I looked up the interview with Mike in *Working*, I found this passage:

> I would like to see a building, say, the Empire State Building, I would like to see on one side of it a foot wide strip from top to bottom with the name of every bricklayer, the name of every electrician, with all the names. So when a guy walked by, he could take his son and say, "See, that's me over there on the forty-fifth floor. I put the steel beam in."

In rewriting I would probably take some of Mike's original language and work it into my own, resulting in something like this:

> Mike, the steelworker, felt that every building should acknowledge, somewhere, the names of all the electricians, steelworkers, bricklayers, and plumbers who worked on it.

A FINAL NOTE

It is probably obvious that rewrites such as the one above are as much revising as editing. There isn't a hard and fast line between the two activities. When I write I sometimes compose, revise, and edit almost simultaneously, which is fine as long as the work gets done. Hard and fast rules for writing at any stage in the process simply don't exist.

The last part of this book focuses on writing as a research activity. Chapter 13 explains the basic elements of research; Chapter 14 describes a particular kind of journal called a research log; Chapter 15 examines living resources in everyone's community; Chapter 16 examines the research library; and Chapter 17 outlines the use of references and footnotes in writing research papers.

SUGGESTIONS FOR JOURNAL WRITING

1. How do you compose? See if you can reconstruct the process by which you wrote your last paper: What did you do first? second?

In what ways does your composing process resemble that described in this chapter? in what ways differ?

2. Select any paragraph from this chapter and see if some editing could improve it. (I've come to believe almost any text—certainly my own—can be made tighter, stronger, more effective by careful editing.)

3. Keep your journal on a word processor for a week. Do you think it makes any difference in the thoughts you write? In the way you put your thoughts?

SUGGESTIONS FOR ESSAY WRITING

1. Write an essay on writing an essay. Use yourself as a model and see if you can explain some of the process of writing that, for most of us, remains a constant mystery.

2. Attach to the next essay you write for this class a record of how it was written: Where did the idea come from? How many drafts did you write? at what time of day? Would you identify discrete stages in the process of its composition? (You could do this best if you kept a log documenting each time you did anything related to completing this essay.)

SUGGESTIONS FOR RESEARCH PROJECTS

1. **INDIVIDUAL:** Investigate the composing process of one of your favorite writers. Check the library to find out whether he or she has ever been interviewed or written an essay or letters on how he or she writes. (See, for example, the *Paris Review* anthologies, in which writers talk about their writing.) Then look closely at some of this writer's work and see if you can find any examples of this process in action. Write a Composing Profile of this writer, supporting your findings with examples from the writer's publications.

2. **COLLABORATIVE:** Locate teachers in your school who are serious writers and interview them. Do they write only after they have all of their data? Do they keep journals or logs of the process? How would they identify the steps or stages or phases of their own processes? Share interview data and write, individually or as small-group teams, a Resource Guide to Composing documented with the interview data collected.

Part III

WRITING
AND RESEARCH

Chapter 13

FINDING RESEARCH QUESTIONS

Research, as a process, is exploratory, not scientific.

James Kinneavy, *A Theory of Discourse*. Prentice Hall, 1971, p. 79.

Authentic research begins with yourself, when you ask questions and look for answers. In looking, you pose more questions, talk to people, dig in libraries, and try one method then another. It's not easy, but it's sometimes fun. And always *you* are present, the guiding curiosity and controlling intelligence, trying to find something out.

THE RESEARCH PAPER

Many years ago, when I was required to write a research paper in first-year English, I didn't know what a research paper was or could become. As a result, the assignment bewildered me, and my paper was a disaster. I had troubles, not because research is necessarily difficult (though sometimes it is), but because of the way I approached it—as formulaic and routine. Despite what my English instructor told me—that I should investigate any current issue in which I was truly interested—I approached the task with the preconception that such writing left no room for imagination, creativity, or personality. In other words, I worried so much about the rules that I imagined governed research writing, I made no room in the assignment for what I really cared about. That was a mistake.

The topic I finally set out to investigate was capital punishment—a topic suggested by my instructor in response to the utterly blank look on my face, reflecting my totally blank state of mind. To write the paper, I followed the recommended procedure as outlined by both teacher and handbook. It went something like this:

> (1) Search the card catalogue in the library for pertinent books on capital punishment; (2) Search the *Reader's Guide to Periodical Literature* for relevant popular articles; (3) Search the *Social Science Index*; (4) make bibliographic cards (3 × 5) identifying sources consulted; (5) Make note cards (4 × 6) on which to copy quotations and notes from what you read; (6) Write out the thesis statement on capital punishment (probably pro or con, but I no longer remember which it was); (7) Make an outline of the whole paper; (8) Type the paper; (9) Cite sources with footnotes and bibliography following the guidelines of the Modern Language Association (MLA).

This is what I remember, but I probably missed a few steps, like getting teacher approval of my note cards and handing in the outline a week in advance of the due date, but you get the point. The nine steps outlined here summarize my misconception of what a research paper was all about. In fact, if you've never written such a paper yourself, and you follow these routine steps, you'll be able to write one and probably earn at least a "C" for your effort. The only difference between my tedious paper of twenty-five years ago and the tedious one these steps would lead you to write today is the change in MLA reference form.

A PROBLEM TO SOLVE

I'd like to tell you about a car I bought recently, a new Saab 900. Actually, I'd like to tell you about the buying of the car rather than the car itself. I think you'll find this interesting.

I live in Vermont and have owned front-wheel drive Saabs, which are especially good in snow, for some time. But my eight-year-old Saab 99, which my 16-year-old daughter affectionately dubbed the "granola" car because of its spotty brown color, was clearly showing signs of age—mainly rust. For about a year I had been casually looking at newer cars, but sometime in October, when the dealers began discounting last year's new cars to make room for next year's new cars, I began to get serious about replacing—or at least supplementing—the granola car.

Here is how I went about buying my new car:

1. One Sunday, with my daughter, I visited P.J.'s Auto Village to look at new Saabs (I went on a Sunday because the dealer was closed and I could look without making even a modest

commitment to a salesperson that I was interested in buying something).

2. That Sunday afternoon, we visited other dealers as well, checking out the competition; I found myself interested in Honda Accords, Toyota Camrys, and Volkswagen Jettas, in addition to Saabs.

3. I read *Consumer Reports* magazine, to which I subscribe: *CU* reported that the Saab 900 is a safe, solid, reliable, and unusual car—which maintained my interest in Saabs.

4. I visited the Brownell Library, near my house, and looked up road tests of the four cars in which I was interested in both *Popular Mechanics* and *Road and Track*; they all looked good.

5. I visited my Saab dealer again, this time when it was open, and talked with a salesman about price and options on a new Saab. I also asked about the trade-in value of the granola car (not much).

6. I called Stan, a neighbor who is also a mechanic, and asked if there were any problems with Saab's new sixteen-valve engine. He said it had been out for three years in Sweden, time for the bugs to be worked out.

7. I talked to my tax accountant about my finances, wondering whether or not I could really afford a new car now: she said what accountants usually say, that it was up to me.

8. I reviewed the going prices of used Saabs in a used car buyers guide, browsed in, not purchased, at a local bookstore. I found my present Saab already too old to be listed (not a good sign).

9. I talked to Honda, Toyota, and Volkswagen dealers about options, prices, and trade-ins. But while these cars were all safe, solid, and reliable (and cheaper), they weren't "unusual."

10. I returned to P.J.'s and bought the new Saab 900 without trading in the granola car, which pleased my sixteen-year-old, because it was she who had named it and would now get to drive it.

I suppose I have skipped a few steps here, like reading the want ads in the *Burlington Free Press*, watching the new car ads on television with special interest, and having long debates with my wife about middle-class and middle-age values.

Why do I tell you about buying a car in a chapter on research writing? Because buying a car, or a bike, or a stereo, or a house, is a research project—a real one with unpleasant consequences for not doing your homework carefully. You may know what I mean if you've had to research which college to attend, which subject to major in, which career to pursue, or which city to live in. People conduct research of one sort or another whenever they need information they don't currently possess. People research to answer questions, to solve problems, and to make informed decisions—and they do such research in their private lives and on the job more often than for college term-paper assignments.

As you can see, in buying a car, it didn't matter whether I wrote research notes on 3×5 cards (which I didn't), in my journal (which I did), on dealer brochures (which I also did), or on napkins (which I didn't). What mattered was the substance of the search: that I bought one car rather than another, got a good buy, and was happy with what I bought. The whole search-and-buy process took about a month; what sustained me was my personal interest in the topic (I like to talk and read about good cars) and my personal investment in the outcome (I like to drive good cars as well as talk and read about them).

Buying a car is both similar to and different from being told to write a college research paper. The similarity is mainly in the method; the difference, in the personal investment. However, I'd like to convince you that it may be worth investing considerably more of yourself in your college research projects—even those rigidly assigned—than I did as a first-year college student.

WHY RESEARCH ASSIGNMENTS

Let's look more closely at the reasons why research papers—or term papers, or formal reports—are a major staple in the academic diet. At their best, such assignments ask you to think seriously about what interests you, to formulate questions you care about, to begin poking around in places (both familiar and arcane) for answers or solutions, to master some method for taking and organizing notes, to integrate fragments of knowledge into a meaningful conceptual framework, and to compose the whole business into a coherent report that answers the questions you originally posed—which task, itself, brings to bear all of your accumulated rhetorical skills.

Any assignment that asks you to perform the variety of activities outlined here might justly be considered central to what learning is all about. As you perform these activities for the first time, you may find them difficult. However, as you become better at them—better at investigating, conceptualizing, criticizing, and writing—research will get easier and you'll have a good time. In short, good, open-ended research assignments taken seriously—unlike my freshman report on capital punishment—make you a more agile, careful, and tough thinker, as well as give you practice communicating that agility, care, and toughness to others.

ASKING QUESTIONS
Why

Research implies finding an answer to a question or solution to a problem that puzzles you. It also implies that you care what the answer or solution is. Finally, research implies a process or method of looking that varies from field to field. In science research we call this method "scientific" and employ microscopes, computers, telescopes, and test tubes to help us find answers; in the humanities, we might call it criticism and usually confine ourselves to the study of texts. The point is that along with having a question, we also need a method for answering, one that we trust to yield useful knowledge or numbers.

Where

To find answers, we need to know *where* to look. Buying a car depends on seeing, reading about, and test driving a car. However, school research projects most commonly rely on reading, writing, and experimenting in libraries or laboratories.

Who

Research implies a searcher, someone to pose questions, formulate hypotheses (hunches), look for and test solutions—a person who, in many science experiments, is supposed to be out of sight, but who in the humanities might well be center stage in the experiment, like Mike Wallace skillfully questioning reluctant witnesses on *60 Minutes* or Sherlock Holmes injecting his analytical intelligence into a muddle of disparate clues. In all cases, however, whether covertly or overtly, the intelligence of the researcher is the controlling force that guides the search for solution. This understanding, that the researcher must be in control, as a master interrogator or detective, is crucial to giving the research project integrity, dignity, and worth.

To return briefly to my car-buying example, you will notice the sources to which I quite naturally turned in my quest for information: (1) I talked to people, both friends and experts; (2) I visited several sites to see for myself; and (3) I read books and periodicals—found at home, in bookstores, and in libraries. Essentially, these are the same resources researchers in any field use to find answers to questions: people, places, and printed words.

SUGGESTIONS FOR JOURNAL WRITING

1. What has been your past experience in writing research papers? What topics did you investigate? Why? Was the result something you cared about? Did you learn something worthwhile? Did you receive a good grade? Describe what most interested you about the project, what most turned you off.

2. Re-create the steps of the process you went through the last time you researched something on your own: Where did you start? Whom did you talk to? What sites did you investigate? What were some of the outcomes?

3. If you had your druthers, what topics would you choose to research right now: an issue you care about? a place you'd like to visit? something you'd like to buy? Write a paragraph or so on several of these and see what kind of questions you actually have.

SUGGESTIONS FOR ESSAY WRITING

1. Imagine that you are giving a talk to ninth or tenth graders at the high school from which you graduated. Your topic is how to make research more exciting: write the talk drawing examples from your own personal experience as a researcher.

2. Select an essay you wrote sometime in this course and add a research dimension to it. In other words, talk to someone, go someplace, or read something that will add more authority to this previously undocumented piece of writing. For example, if you wrote a personal essay about working at McDonald's, go back there and collect more information, observations, and interviews, and work this data into your original paper to give it increased credibility.

3. Select one of the topics from Journal Suggestion #3 and write about it as best you can, right now, using no outside research. (Then, of course, pursue it further, following Research Suggestion #3 below, thereby turning this essay into a discovery draft.)

SUGGESTIONS FOR RESEARCH PROJECTS

1. **INDIVIDUAL:** Investigate the research process of some favorite, famous researcher in any field (e.g., Thomas Jefferson, Thomas

Edison, Margaret Mead, Jonas Salk, Shirley Brice Heath, George Plimpton, Hunter S. Thompson, John McPhee, others). Report your results in a technical report format (see Chapter 8).

2. **COLLABORATIVE:** It is likely that some professors in each department on your campus are well known for their research. Interview them and compile your findings into a "Resource Guide to College Research" for prospective majors in the different disciplines represented in your guide. Write an introduction pointing out similarities and differences among the processes and methods of the researchers interviewed.

3. Continue to pursue your own research project as perhaps begun under "Journal" and "Essay Suggestions #3" above. Keep track of your progress (both good leads and dead ends) in a "Research Log" (see next chapter). Report your results to the class in a report that blends your personal enthusiasm with the more concrete results of your investigation.

Chapter 14

THE RESEARCH LOG

10/14 I reread John's comments about my paper. He's right, I need to add more about the 1930's and 40's. He also mentioned a letter from Einstein to the President which I never heard of. I'll have to find out about that. I think I need chronological order instead of subject order—and I need a better opening. Also I want to put more of my voice into it.

[Lisa]

The above entry is taken from the log Lisa used to keep track of her research project for her college English class. This entry was written after she had shared her first three-page paper draft with a classmate and received back his written critique. In this chapter, we will look at a special kind of journal called a research log, which documents your daily journey from class to the card catalogue to the library stacks to the pile of notes on your desk. From the time you begin a research project through the final draft of your completed typed manuscript, this log collects your starts and stops, questions and answers, notes, speculations, and doubts—just like any journal, except here, you maintain a single focus on one project. Of course, an easy way to keep a research log is to partition off the back section of your journal or class notebook, keeping all of your course records together.

If you write daily in the log, you improve your chances of both finding and catching insights, which, of course, you will need to write insightful papers. Most serious writers use something like a log to help them start and then monitor the development of major writing and research projects. Broadly interpreted, research logs can be about any thoughts you have while doing your research.

Your log will provide a place to monitor the progress of a given piece of writing, to evaluate emerging drafts, and to discuss with yourself strategies for further revision and editing. While logs and journals will usually be in the background in a class, you will find them useful in keeping the foreground writing strong and on course.

In addition, I've spoken with a number of reference librarians about how they help college students who are writing research papers. They believe that students who come to the library to *start* their research projects waste great amounts of time, their own and the librarian's. They believe it is far better for students to do some writing about what they want to research and why *before* approaching the card catalogue or *Reader's Guide*. A perfect use for the research log is starting your project by asking yourself a series of questions and writing out some tentative answers. Here are some initial questions:

1. On what subject do I want to spend time reading and researching?
2. What do I already know about this subject?
3. What question or questions do I want to answer?
4. Can I break my general question into a series of more specific questions?
5. Who can I talk to who knows something about this?

If you begin with questions such as these, you might even show some of your answers to the librarians you ask to help you; they especially enjoy helping students who seem to know what they are looking for and why. (Chapters 15, 16, and 17 will provide you with more specific information on writing research papers.)

To illustrate this point, I've borrowed Lisa's research log and reproduced selected entries that focus tightly on one research writing assignment. Lisa kept this log in a first-year composition class at the University of Vermont to document her progress in writing a research paper on Albert Einstein. Let's see how she uses it.

FIRST IMPRESSIONS

Lisa's initial interest in writing about Albert Einstein came from reading an article by Banesh Hoffman, "My Friend Albert Einstein," in the anthology assigned for the course. The article altered Lisa's initial impression of Einstein as a mythical twentieth-century scientist to that of a human being who married (twice), raised children, and mowed the lawn. Her first reaction to Hoffman's ideas recorded on the first day of October begins as follows:

> I had a preconceived image of him being so scientific and mechanical. Uptight and bookwormish. However Banesh Hoffman showed Albert Einstein in a completely different light. That interests me, because it's a side we don't normally see in historical figures— especially scientists & Nobel Prize winners. We see only their contributions & none of their personalities or the reasons behind their contributions. He is someone I'd love to get to know now.

Lisa confronts her earlier stereotypes of Einstein and finds them wanting. In response, she locates a point of personal interest— Einstein's personality—and decides that *that* part of history seems worthy of further exploration. In this case, the journal seems merely to document the writer's starting point. Actually it does more than this, because the very process of recording those initial impressions also pushes them a little further: Einstein becomes someone Lisa would "love to get to know."

ASSUMPTIONS

Whenever you tackle a new job or assignment, you start out with certain beliefs and assumptions, which may be reinforced, modified or abandoned as your work progresses. Log writing can be helpful, because as you write out your assumptions, you become aware of what they are, increasing the chances of doing something productive with them. Lisa's next log entry, two days later (10/3), reveals her uncertainty about herself as a student of history:

> I don't know anything about history—it's my worst subject & it puts me to great disadvantage when it comes to writing or thinking about people in the past—it's out of context. . . . Anyway, I assume both wars went on during his life. The Nazis and Hitler & holocaust, Hitler torturing the Jews & later in his life maybe the WW II w/ Japanese bombing Pearl Harbor.

In this entry, Lisa reveals some confusion about the two World Wars that dominated the first half of the twentieth century. Although she realizes that Einstein was involved with both of them, she seems to believe that the war with Germany was a different one from the war with Japan. Lisa's uncertainties will lead to her first questions because she must check out her own preconceptions. She does seem to need help with history, yet I wonder if she is as ignorant about history as she believes she is.

FIRST QUESTIONS

Curiosity is the necessary precondition to writing well about anything: the more questions you have, the more likely you are to pursue answers; the more answers you have, the more you have to write about. The log is a good place to practice asking questions, first to yourself, later to the card catalogue, *Reader's Guide*, etc. In the log, especially, there is no penalty for not knowing something, as there may be in a formal paper or examination. The log is also a place to keep a record of the questions you are pursuing, and to witness how writing one question down often inspires yet another.

On 10/7, about a week after her initial investigation of Einstein, Lisa writes about what else she wants and needs to know about him:

> I need to know more of the things which influenced him. His personal life, when he was younger, his young adulthood, his family, etc.
>
> Also the events going on in Germany & Europe in general. I believe this has an influence on his ideas & personality. I'd like to be able to fit him into history & see him in his time.
>
> I'd like to see what people of his time thought of him & how he related to them. I'm interested in the image given by Banesh Hoffman because it makes Einstein seem like such a real person— I'd like to know if other people saw him in the same way or if he was "untouchable" because of his fame & brilliance.
>
> I guess my question continues to be what he was like as a person, & how his early life was influenced to make him such a genius.

FOCUSED QUESTIONS

As Lisa pursued her questions, she recorded what she found in her research log and asked still more-focused questions. This jotting activity can be an important kind of entry, as lists of questions allow the writer to see the range of possible topics to pursue further. Below, on 10/10, Lisa recorded the following fragments and questions:

> —Used the library today, need more on what influenced him.
> —need to read his essay in book to hear his voice
> —more on personality

—check dates & places (schools, jobs)
—find out what religion and beliefs
—family
—try to focus my paper more, maybe not just life and young adult-
  hood, but how it affected his future, fame, genius
—relate personality to how he became brilliant or known
—did he relate as well to others as he did to science?

Here, the log serves as a catch-all for her scattered questions about her research project as well as a prod to keep her going in certain directions. (When I make such lists in my journal, I commonly return to them and check them off, or cross out the questions that have ceased to interest me. As discussed in Chapter 3, the journal or log is simply a place where you can methodically record problem-solving activities.)

RESEARCHING

Before Lisa ever started a draft of her actual research paper, she worked out what she knew and what she didn't. We find this entry for 10/13:

> I know little about the beginning of WWI [or] what was going on
> before. I do know that he's very against WW II & outspoken
> w/ his beliefs. He's a pacifist.

It's difficult to tell if she's discovered the differences between the two World Wars yet, but she's clearly attending to Einstein's involvement in World War II. Although she doesn't reveal a lot here, it's important for the log writer simply to keep going, recording even little bits and pieces to keep the research momentum alive. The incessant presence of the log (perhaps coupled with some insistence from the instructor) ensures that the research project is not dropped until the day the paper is due.

PLANNING

Lisa's teacher asked her to write a discovery draft before actually beginning a formal draft of the paper. The purpose, of course, was to discover how the information was coming together and whether some controlling ideas were emerging that could actually structure her paper. (At this point, students exchanged papers and critiqued them for each other, resulting in the entry of 10/14 reprinted at the head of this chapter.)

On 10/15, Lisa records in her log how she moved from discovery to first draft:

> I merely changed the order & reworded sentences & paragraphs. Everything was moved around. I tried to fill in left out information, but when I reread, I realize a lot is still missing. I like this order much better & now I can fill in things easier & in a more organized fashion.

Lisa's discovery draft was three pages long; her first full draft was five. In addition to moving things around, she's imparting missing information—helped by a classmate's reading and her own sense of what's missing as she attempts to write a paper that will sound knowledgeable. The log is useful here to help her become aware of her growth as a writer, a process more important in the long run than the development of her Einstein paper.

EVALUATING

On 10/16, Lisa, apparently pleased with the organization but not with the tone of her language, has further thoughts about this initial draft:

> I'm not happy w/ the way the paper sounds. It doesn't seem to flow right. It's almost as if it has more than one voice—many voices. . . . I'm not working on the first draft today however.

She's right. In looking at her first draft, we find a tone more typical of an encyclopedia than that of an eager research writer. Here are a few sentences from her opening paragraph:

> Albert Einstein was born on March 14, 1879 in Ulm, Germany, as the first child of Pauline and Hermann Einstein. Shortly after, he and his parents moved to Munich. Einstein never liked school or did well in it. He disliked the rigidity of the Catholic school he attended.

Lisa isn't happy with her voice because she's just patched it together from different sources. What's important is that she knows it, records it in her log, and works to change it. With this kind of self-tutorial, Lisa will grow as a writer.

REVISING

On 10/18, Lisa has again visited the library and also begun to revise her first draft:

> I found another book that gives me a little more insight to his life. I reworded a lot because it made no sense & sounded childish & dry—no voice, just facts. I still need a better intro and conclusion.

It is now two and a half weeks into the Einstein project, and Lisa's log shows entries nearly every day. Here, she mentions again her dissatisfaction with the voice in the paper, but because she's talking more to herself than to her instructor, she doesn't fill us in on what, exactly, she found childish. This is a good time for Lisa to have a one-to-one conference with her writing teacher.

MORE READING

On 10/20, Lisa writes:

> I wouldn't say I felt like a historian, but I found the best book today, Einstein: Profile of the Man. The author interviews Einstein's son & wrote the most personal account of his life. . . . I'm used to essays that go over my head or dry encyclopedia articles—packed w/ facts w/ no personality. Just by flipping through the book & reading a page here & there, I found a goldmine of information.

She is aware here that she still isn't behaving as a historian would; however, to make that observation, she obviously knows something about what historians do. In fact, I'd guess that she *is* beginning to feel like an historian, despite her disclaimer—an especially important development when compared to her attitude on 10/3, where she professed, "I don't know anything about history."

FINISHING

It's now about three weeks since Lisa began to work on the research project for her writing class. During that time, she not only wrote several drafts of the paper itself, but fifteen separate log entries documenting her thinking about it. On 10/20, she writes:

> Today I copied 1st draft over including notes added on the side. It's getting much longer & I'm quite happy with it. It seems like one whole thing now, instead of facts. Profile of the Man helped a lot

getting my mind and the paper in the right order. I can relate the facts to each other much better now. I still have no conclusion—I didn't like the other one.

At this point Lisa's research log stops. The rest of her energy on this project went into finishing the paper she had now worked on for three weeks. Her log had been a tool to work through the process of writing the paper; once the paper was finished, the log itself became a historical document. Her final paper opens with some of the same material, but in a voice that seems more confidently Lisa's own:

> As a boy, Einstein never really liked school nor did very well in it. He disliked the rigidity of the Catholic school and was bored with the study of language and history. But he loved science.

I learned from her teacher that Lisa received a B + on the final paper, a fourth draft. Although the log doesn't guarantee a perfect final product, it does guarantee continual and methodical attention to the project, significantly increasing the project's chances of success.

You have probably noticed throughout the log entries that Lisa's language was informal, reading very much as if she were talking casually among friends. You will also notice that from time to time she makes a reference to something we don't fully understand, such as parts of her paper or books she is finding. We who are eavesdropping on her log need to remember that it is written essentially for herself—with the understanding that her teacher, too, will see it from time to time. We are the audience she never anticipated.

SUGGESTIONS FOR JOURNAL WRITING

1. Keep a research log (separate from your normal class journal in some way) for three or four weeks about whatever subject interests you. Note there all of your preconceptions, hunches, theories, tentative conclusions, good leads, and false starts.

2. Keep a log for several weeks about one of your hobbies (photography, stamp collecting), sports (soccer, running), or activities (volunteer day care work, student government). (If you're as busy with school work as I imagine, some of these will be easier to do only after this course is completed—still, it's a good suggestion.)

3. Keep a research log for a writing project you are doing for another class—whether or not the instructor requires it. When you have

finished the paper, evaluate the contribution your log entries made toward your final product.

SUGGESTIONS FOR ESSAY WRITING

1. Carefully examine your research log (see #1 above) and write an introduction explaining the research process you find there.

2. Write an essay in which some research and investigation are necessary. When you write this "research essay," include a running commentary on the process of your research as well as the product of it. (For more information on essays such as this see Ken Macrorie's *I Search*, Heinemann, 1988.)

SUGGESTIONS FOR RESEARCH PROJECTS

1. **INDIVIDUAL:** Keep a research log about a topic you are investigating, noting (a) your initial hunches and speculations, (b) the useful resources you locate, and (c) all the false starts, dead ends, and missing resources you find as you pursue your research. Complete your project, write an imaginative paper about it, and append to it this log.

2. **COLLABORATIVE:** Exchange your research log with another student in class, and analyze what you find there: Can you find germinal hunches? leaps of faith? evidence of methodical procedure? Report your findings first to your classmate, check your hunches with him or her, then write an analysis of him or her as a researcher, documenting your hunches with evidence drawn from the log.

Chapter 15

RESOURCES: PEOPLE AND PLACES

PEOPLE

Start with people. When you need to find something out, start asking around and see who knows what. People are living, current resources that talk back, smile, and surprise you. People can tell you who else to see, where to go, what books to read (and why); people can offer you shortcuts. They can also ask you questions: Why do you want to do this? What do you expect to find? Have you talked to Professor Smith yet? How far back do you want to go? Where do you plan to start?

Wherever you live, there are people who know more than you do about all kinds of things. It's your job as a researcher to discover these people and find out what they know. When you talk to people, you are in much the same situation as a newspaper reporter interviewing people to complete a story. In fact, you can learn a lot about interviewing people from investigative reporters. Here are some ideas that might help you collect information directly from people.

Expect Something

Good interviewers aren't blank slates. They talk to people to find out more about something about which they already have some ideas and hunches. In other words, they start with preconceptions, and then go on to prove or disprove them. When they talk to people, they are actively looking for answers, and they have some idea of the shape those answers will take. Acknowledging this, being aware of what you expect and why, will help you both to form pointed questions and to change, modify, or adapt your expectations when something unexpected comes along.

Hang Around

I can't improve on the advice of Bill Blundel, columnist for the *Wall Street Journal*, who said, "To my way of thinking there's no such thing as a cowboy expert. The only cowboy expert is the cowboy. And the only way you can find out and appreciate what his life is like is to work with him, and to go out with him and to be there, just hanging around. I am a tremendous believer in just hanging around."

Know Something

Before you talk to knowledgeable people, become knowledgeable yourself. Even before you "start with people," check in a dictionary, encyclopedia, or newspaper to learn the terms that will help you ask good questions. Sometimes this means asking people about other people to talk to. For those other people, of whom you expect something particular, it may mean familiarizing yourself with their writing, their achievements, their expertise in general. Keep in mind that you'll get one kind of information if you present yourself as a novice and another kind when you appear already knowledgeable. The second kind will be deeper and more useful.

Plan Questions

Prepare a few key questions in advance. This doesn't mean you should interview from a study sheet, although some people do. Writing out the questions helps you both find and remember them. Think about the nature and sequence of questions you ask. One approach is to start with a general question: "How did you get involved with the problem of homeless people in the first place?" Then ask a narrowing question: "What services do you currently provide for the homeless?" And follow-up questions as the occasion provides: "How long have you been doing that?" Sometimes a provocative leading question will provide interesting information: "According to the Mayor, your homeless shelter is not providing the services promised." And sometimes an imaginative approach will help: "If you were the Mayor, what's the first thing you'd do to deal with the problem of the homeless?" In other words, I try to rehearse in my head what will happen if I lead with one question rather than another, try to predict what I'll get for an answer, and then see if that's the direction I want to go. I do all of this on paper, to myself, imagining, before I go into the actual interview.

Ad Lib Questions

No matter what my plans, in my best interviews, I never follow them. Good interviews move around considerably, include digressions (often loaded with information that circles back and becomes useful), and are refreshingly unpredictable. So I also plan for both new and follow-up questions as part of my interview: by planning to ad lib I'm not tied to my script and can follow a new lead wherever it seems most fruitful: "What, exactly, do you mean by that?" "Could you expand on that just a bit more?" "I really hadn't thought about that before." "What else should I know?" Remember, it's the prepared questions that help you identify when it's time for the other kind!

Ask Leading Questions

If you have expectations, theories, and ideas, sometimes you might lead off with them and see what your interviewee thinks. It depends on who you are talking to. For example, if you are investigating overcrowded conditions at your local airport, the parking lot attendant will have a different stake in the matter than a cab driver, and the airport manager will have a view quite different from the resident across the street. To whom do you ask what leading question? With whom do you wait to see if the subject of overcrowding comes up? Play your hunches and see what happens.

Use Silence

This may be difficult, but it's profitable. Silence is awkward, and many of us have a natural tendency to fill it. But silence means different things at different times: sometimes ignorance, confusion, or hostility; other times thinking, feeling, or remembering. Wherever you can, allow the person some silence and see what happens. If it's hostile silence, you'll soon know it. But it is more likely that the person is doing some mental collecting and will fill the silences directly. Often, such silence can draw out rich information you never expected.

Repeat Assertions

In scanning your notes at the end of an interview, it's a good idea to repeat some of the points you find most useful and plan to use in your paper. Repeating what you believe to have heard can save you later embarrassment. You can both double-check your notes for accuracy, which is crucial if you're asking someone about a sensitive issue, and often get additional insights that have been incubating as you talked.

Tape Recording

Sometimes you want to record exactly what someone says to you, so you ask if you can tape the conversation. Sounds easy. But the trade-off for accuracy is sometimes extra nervousness for both of you and a lot of time spent playing and transcribing what you've recorded. Many good reporters, even when they have a tape recorder as backup, take quick but careful notes in a steno-pad (small, flips fast, easy to write on your lap). It helps to devise a few shorthand tricks— abbreviations for common terms, initials where clear, and standard symbols like "w/" and "&." The notes taken right there also serve to remind you about what was said both during the interview and later; having the pen in your hand helps you jot out further questions as your subject is speaking. Even if you tape, make your pen and paper work for you.

PLACES

Physical settings may play an important part in your research project. When you visit actual places where events happen or information is located, you experience your information in a way that's different than if you only read about it. Interviews, for instance, are often enhanced by reporting on the physical place where it takes place: What does the person's office look like? What's on the walls? What books are on the shelves? And so on. In the pages that follow are some additional ideas for extracting information from places.

Stop

Go to places and observe what is there. Investigate local issues and institutions to find out what investigative research is like. Stop and look inside the church, sit in the pews, and note what you feel. Go stand on the Brooklyn Bridge, a hundred feet above the cold, black water of the East River, and look at the city skyline, the ocean horizon. Visit the neighborhood in which the most welfare mothers are said to live and cross its streets and sit in a diner booth and drink a cup of coffee. Stop, pause, get a sense of what this place is like. Sociological reports won't generate that kind of thick information.

In the following example, Ken, a student in my first-year college class, describes his visit to a local dentist to investigate preventive dentistry:

> On entering his office I did not find the long wait, the screaming kids, and the general coldness of so many dentists' offices. Instead I found a small warm waiting room with carpeted floors, soft chairs, and classical music, with copies of *Atlantic Monthly* along with *Sports Illustrated* on the coffee table.

Look

Careful description is part of good research. The writer who is able to observe people, events, and places, and to convey that observation accurately contributes factual information to the research process. Such careful description of place establishes living, colorful, memorable contexts for all sorts of other inquiries. Look closely at the obvious and see what else is there. Go for the size, scale, color, light, texture, angle, order and disorder, smell and taste of the place. Use your senses to find out what's there—and use your language to convey it to others. Go to the places close at hand, the library, bookstore, or student union; practice recording what you find there. Try first to record in neutral language, suppressing as much as possible your own bias; next add—or delete—your bias and give what you see as some personal color. Which seems more effective? Why?

When you interview people—on the street, in a coffee shop, in their home or office—look for clues that tell you something about the individuals. In what office, what company, what neighborhood does each one work? Researchers train themselves to look closely and take good notes so they have a context for their information. Looking and recording are the essence of research.

In the following example, Susan describes her visit to the student newspaper office:

> My eyes wander around the room as we talk. . . . One thing arouses my curiosity: on the pegboards between the large desks hang rolls of tape. All kinds, shapes and sizes of tape: big rolls, small rolls, thick rolls, thin rolls, full rolls, nearly empty rolls. Rows of electrical tape, duct tape, masking tape, and Scotch tape.

What does the tape say about a newspaper office? That a lot of patching goes on? Does the tape symbolize the endless need to connect and put together that is the essence of newspaper production? Making the note enables her later to use it or not, depending on the slant of her story. If she didn't have the note, neither would she have the option of using it. Take copious notes.

Listen

Wherever you go as an observer, you are also a listener: keep your ears open when drinking that cup of coffee; listen to the small talk in the airport lobby; record what you hear whenever you can. A writer sometimes finds the lead vignette for a story in some overheard snatch of conversation. Remember that research papers are essentially stories.

One of my students started her report on Evangel Baptist Church by visiting the church, which was located across the street from the unversity. The following is her lead paragraph:

> The people around me were wearing everything from three piece suits to flannel shirts, jeans, and tennis shoes. I was surprised how loud everyone was talking, laughing, and joking before the sermon. "What *happened* last night?" "*Nothing* I can tell you *here*."

Experiment

Design situations that will help you discover new information. Some of my students have conducted simple experiments that provide them with original data and firsthand knowledge. For example, in an early draft, one of my students stated that all biology majors are really "pre-med students" because her two roommates happened to be biology majors with such a focus. I challenged her on this point, so she conducted a formal survey of a large introductory biology class— and found out that many students were pre-med, but 39 percent were not! She then had information to back up whatever point she wanted to make in her paper.

In a similar vein, instead of arguing that women enroll in engineering curricula primarily "to find husbands" (!), find out how many students in the graduating class are women, and report carefully the results. Instead of saying that automobiles never stop at the stop sign at the foot of Beacon Street, sit there for a morning and record full stops, rolling stops, and no stops for a period of two hours; then you can say something based on direct knowledge.

Even simple experiments can yield useful data once you determine that such data might make you more of an authority once you understand how to collect it. There is a vast literature on designing surveys and questionnaires, but a professor in the social or educational sciences might be able to show you some shortcuts or information aimed at lay researchers.

Write

Don't spend too long visiting, interviewing, describing, and collecting without writing. Your collected information will make little sense until you force it to do so, and writing does that. Try not to spend forever making still more notes on 3 × 5 cards, shuffling and reshuffling to find the best order. All that stuff is useful, but remember that one of the best ways to see how your material is or isn't fitting together is to start writing about it. All your book notes, recordings, site descriptions, statistics, quotations, and theories only begin to make sense when you can see them in some kind of relationship with one another and watch the pattern they take.

Finally, whatever the subject of your investigation, the actual report you write can take many possible shapes, depending on how you formulate your questions about it. Consider, for example, the following lead paragraphs of three different writers who jointly investigated the minimum security Chittenden Community Correctional Center in Burlington, Vermont. Although they shared information throughout the project and visited the jail together, each wrote a distinctly different report.

> Walking up to the door of the Chittenden Community Correctional Center made me feel a bit on edge. The inmates were staring at us; I just wanted to leave. As Debbie put it, "Six girls in a Correctional Center at 8:00 p.m., I must be nuts."
>
> [Lydia]

> Do you ever wonder what goes on behind the doors of a correctional center? What does it offer its inmates to improve their lives? Have you wondered what types of programs the centers provide?
>
> [Jennifer]

> The Chittenden Community Correctional Center is found on Farrell Street, just off Swift Street, not five minutes from the University of Vermont campus. Within its boundaries criminals are serving time for drunk driving, petty theft, and assault and battery.
>
> [Debby]

Each student investigated the same institution and each had a different idea for a lead and, ultimately, a different story to tell. At the same time, each lead proves interesting and invites further reading.

The purpose of this chapter has been to widen the possibilities of college-level research to include places and issues in the local community. The next chapter investigates the research possibilities of the central institution of all colleges and universities, the library.

SUGGESTIONS FOR JOURNAL WRITING

1. Describe your past experiences interviewing people: What made them go smoothly? What was difficult? How does this chapter give you help for future interviews?

2. Describe your classroom in careful detail from memory. Then, next time you are in the classroom, notice how much detail you missed. What does this tell you about remembering versus being there in person?

3. Make a list of ten local places that it would be interesting to visit. Which one is most interesting to you?

4. Make a list of ten social issues that have (or could have) local consequences. Which one is most consequential to you?

5. Make a list of local people to whom you could talk about the issues listed in #4.

SUGGESTIONS FOR RESEARCH ESSAYS

1. **INDIVIDUAL:** Select a site listed in your journal and visit it. Describe it, interview somebody there, and find out if there is an issue to pursue further. If there is, pursue it, keeping a research log to document your way. (Possible places to investigate: public transportation centers, local businesses, government facilities, campus institutions, social agencies, parks, concert halls, malls, museums, schools, and prisons.)

2. **INDIVIDUAL:** Write a profile of a person in your community. Interview this person as well as people who know him or her; describe his or her living environment; let the person speak for himself or herself in your final paper. (For profile models consult *The New Yorker*, *Playboy*, *Reader's Digest*, or *Rolling Stone*.)

3. **COLLABORATIVE:** Select one of the same sites as above, but tackle the project as a group (3–5 members): divide up who visits where, interviews whom, looks up what. Agree to share all resources by typing them up and duplicating them for group members. Finally, write either (a) individual papers, sharing the collective research (and citing each other where appropriate) or (b) one collaborative paper, longer, sharing the writing and editing in some equitable way among you.

4. **COLLABORATIVE:** Select a community of people (e.g., sports team, business associates, academic department, agency workers

and clients) and develop a collective profile (use techniques as in #2 above).

5. **OPEN:** Do any of the projects above and invent an interesting form in which to report your results: a TV script? a feature newspaper story? an exchange of letters? a short book with chapters? a drama? a technical report? a magazine article? a multimedia event?

Chapter 16

RESOURCES: BOOKS
AND PERIODICALS

Books are the best things well used, abused among the worst.

Ralph Waldo Emerson

Until now we have focused on the words you write as you learn and demonstrate your learning to others. However, in this chapter, we will focus on the words of others, that are bound in books and periodicals and that remain the primary mode of learning in the academic community.

The library itself is the absolute center of the academic community. Spend time there, get to know it, and the community will take you in. If you need more information about libraries than you find in this brief chapter, consult your local reference librarians—themselves the most useful, knowledgeable, and helpful guides to libraries that exist. Every time I forget something vital about an index, they are there to remind me.

BOOKS AT HOME

When you need information, remember the abundance of resources close at hand. Books, magazines, newspapers, and photocopies are everywhere. You and your friends have collected, informally, dozens of reference works that serve wonderfully as research starters: encyclopedias, dictionaries, handbooks, histories, atlases, anthologies, maps, tour guides, and telephone directories. At the least, these at-hand resources can help you define terms, narrow and compare topics, and provide overview information to get a research project

160

off the ground. In short, collect and become familiar with your own reference resources.

In my own library, which has developed haphazardly over the years since high school and college, I find *Bartlett's Familiar Quotations*, *Roget's Pocket Thesaurus*, *Dictionary of the Bible*, *The Reader's Encyclopedia of Literature*, two *Time-Life* series (one on photography and the other on animals), the *Rand McNally World Atlas*, *The Hammond Road Atlas*, *The World Almanac for 1980*, *The Book of Lists*, cookbooks, home improvement books, and hundreds of paperbacks on literary, historical, social, scientific, and athletic matters—including golf, fishing, photography, and philosophy. My bookshelves have become my first and most readily available library.

In addition, I have several dictionaries, including various editions of *Webster's New World*, *Webster's Collegiate*, *The American Heritage*, and *The Random House*. My own encyclopedia is the one-volume *Columbia*—quite dated (1947) but still full of useful information about historical and geographic subjects. Because it was written over forty years ago, it isn't useful for political and current events, except as background. For more current references, I go to the library and consult a more recent edition of any of the good encyclopedias on the market: *Collier's*, *Columbia*, the *Britannica*, or *Americana*.

BOOKS IN THE LIBRARY

In the modern university library you have access to most of the thoughts generated by humans since the invention of the printing press. Libraries provide awesome access to human ideas, knowledge, and culture—usually through the books and periodicals contained therein. Books, while more comprehensive than periodicals, will be at least a year or two out of date when you read them because of the time it takes from complete manuscript to final, edited bound copy. So when you think of the library for research purposes, think of both books and periodicals. In addition, your university may have special collections of documents stored on tape or film: movies, audio and video tapes, photographs, paintings, and the like. Following is an overview of what the library has in store for you.

Guides

In addition to getting to know the reference librarian, you might make acquaintance with the *Guide to Reference Books*, edited by Gordon Sheehy, which is essentially a guide to guidebooks and can tell which more specialized reference books you could consult. With this single source, any of us can find most of the other source locators in the library. After we learn which call numbers are on which floor, the library becomes a friendly, familiar resource.

Periodicals

You probably already know about *The Reader's Guide to Periodical Literature*, a standard resource for locating both popular and specialized material and possibly the most widely used of all library reference materials. In the *Reader's Guide* you can find author, title, and subject for hundreds of magazines dating back to 1900. If you need something earlier than that, you can check *Poole's Index* (1802–1906) or *Nineteenth Century Reader's Guide* (1890–1899).

Indices

To track down more specialized information published in particular professional or academic journals, you will need to consult one of many other indices, including the *Business Periodicals Index*, the *Social Science Index*, the *Humanities Index*, the *Education Index*, the *Art Index*, *Historical Abstracts* or *Guide to Historical Literature*, *Communication Abstracts*, and *Computer Literature Index*. There are others, but this list suggests the nature and number of library sources that your home bookshelves cannot possibly duplicate.

Card Catalogue

In the card catalogue, you search by either author/title or subject to locate specific books. On index cards in this catalogue, you find the subject of the book; the author's full name, date of birth, and date of death; the date of book publication; the name and location of the publisher; the length in pages and size in inches of the book; and its location in the library (the call number). But card catalogues are not always the last word, especially if their logic does not match yours. For instance, if you want to find out something about World War I but can't find such a listing in the card catalogue, the reference librarian can point you to *The Library of Congress Subject Headings*, which cross-references subject headings and will explain that WWI is called "The Great War" in the card catalogues—a subject heading chosen before history repeated itself in 1939. Keep in mind that good research is a matter of asking good questions and having the persistence to find good answers.

Newspapers

Look also at newspapers with national circulation such as *The New York Times*, *The Wall Street Journal*, and *The Christian Science*

Monitor. These have indices in which you can locate stories about events at the time they happened. After a story is found in *The New York Times* or *The Wall Street Journal* for a certain date, the same date can be checked in the library's collection of local newspapers to see how the event was covered and what local controversy might have been stirred up closer to home.

Computers

Recently, libraries—especially those at major research universities—have begun to make the resources of the library available through computers. In some instances, the card catalogue is now accessible only through a computer keyboard (your own or the library's), which has replaced the familiar wooden file drawers. In addition, numerous libraries now have capabilities for computerized searches (called "on-line" searches) of particular kinds of information. Such searches are conducted according to key words or word combinations that the machine can locate. One of the most frequently used services in my field is called ERIC (Educational Resources Information Center), which provides access to current information—such as papers delivered at professional meetings or proceedings of committees and task forces—even before it appears in periodical or book form. Be careful here: on-line searches may be expensive or restricted (to faculty and graduate students, for instance). In time, this will change, as all libraries will eventually automate the finding of information. For now, ask your librarian what is the best search procedure at your library.

EVALUATING SOURCES

How do you know when a resource is good? Its being in the library is no guarantee that the assertions contained therein are responsible, fair, useful, or relevant to your purposes. The card catalogue won't examine the author's biases, divulge how easy or difficult a book is to read, or offer what experts in the field think about it. For that, you need to check elsewhere—for instance, in the *Book Review Digest* (1905–   ) for the year in which the book was published. In it, you can find a brief overview of what critics thought of the book when it was published and where more complete reviews are located. Indexes such as the *Reader's Guide* also will point to places where the book was reviewed originally.

CRITERIA FOR EVALUATION

What do you do when you want to evaluate a written text but can't find a review of it? Or perhaps the review you find is itself suspect because of that author's extreme bias. The following are some questions to ask of sources new to you:

1. Who is the author? Have you heard of him or her? If so, in what context? Could you find the author's name in another index or encyclopedia?
2. What clues does the title contain about the author's bias or point of view?
3. When was the book or periodical published? If the topic is one on which new information is being rapidly generated, how old can the source be and still be trustworthy?
4. If a book, who published it: A university press? A popular publisher? A specialty publisher? Fly By Night Inc.? Will credibility here be a problem?
5. If an article, where was it published? Do you recognize the periodical? Does it make a difference for credibility if it's in *Reader's Digest*, *Psychology Today*, or *Psychology Abstracts*? How so and to whom?
6. If a book, what can you learn from skimming the table of contents about scope? thesis? direction? strength of authority?
7. Check the reference list or "Works Cited" list at the end of the article, chapters, or volume. Look for names of authors, books, or periodicals that you recognize as respected. If you find none, did you expect to? What does that tell you?
8. Look for signs of use: Has the book been checked out often? Or has it never been checked out? What might that tell you?
9. How long is the piece, chapter, or book? Is length an indication of depth of treatment?
10. Read the first page: What do the words and sentences tell you about tone? Point of view? What does the vocabulary level and sentence length tell you about the audience the author is aiming at?
11. Skim read. Does the author define terms and provide a glossary? Or do you encounter a highly specialized vocabulary and professional jargon unexplained?
12. Look for evidence of evidence. Does the author support assertions with examples? Do you find frequent and substantial documentation?

You also need to know what to do when the library doesn't have a particular book and you don't know when it was published, which means you can't find a review of it. You might then consult *Books in Print*, *Subject Guide to Books in Print*, or *Paperbound Books in*

Print—all of which identify books currently being published, or consult the *Cumulative Book Index*, which will give complete publication data on all books published in the English language. (For foreign authors and titles, consult your reference librarian.)

Finding books and articles is one thing, incorporating them in your writing is quite another. The next chapter will focus on (1) how to use the resources, once found, to substantiate ideas in your own writing and (2) how to document those sources correctly.

SUGGESTIONS FOR JOURNAL WRITING

1. Make a list of library services you want to learn more about. Ask a librarian to help you; record what you learn.

2. Inventory your dorm room, building, apartment, home and list the reference sources already contained therein. Were you surprised by what you found (or didn't)? How so?

3. Select a book at random from your roommate's bookshelf, one you haven't read, and see how much you can learn about it by using the Criteria for Evaluation guidelines in this chapter.

SUGGESTIONS FOR RESEARCH ESSAYS

1. **INDIVIDUAL:** To any of the research ideas suggested in the last few chapters, add a substantial amount of library research: Can you use some of the reference works listed here? Can you include current periodicals as well as books? Will you make sure to look at more than one source?

2. **COLLABORATIVE:** Select an historical subject to research that all members of your group agree upon. Divide up research tasks so that each of you brings back to the group a one- to two-page review of a book and an article to share with the others. Invent an interesting form in which to report the results of your investigation. (See Chapter 17 for appropriate documentation systems.)

Chapter 17

THE USE OF AUTHORITY

Research writing can be only as convincing as the authority that informs it. Remember that every paper you write is an attempt to create belief, to convince your readers that you know what you are talking about and that what you say is true. In personal writing, you persuade your reader that what you say is true by vividly re-creating the images, impressions, and language of your own experience. In research and report writing, however, you persuade also by citing other people's ideas, knowledge, demonstrations, and proofs.

To cite authority doesn't necessarily mean to include long quotations in your writing. In fact, lengthy quotations slow the reader, interrupt the flow of your text, and encourage skim reading. It is more effective to cite experts by paraphrase and summary than by direct quotation. Regardless of which method you use, however, you will need to cite the sources from which you have borrowed. The remainder of this chapter will describe a variety of ways to incorporate expert testimony into your text and how to document that testimony.

DIRECT QUOTATION

If you want to bring an authority into your paper directly, you may need to quote him or her exactly. I use direct quotations when the language of the quotation is especially strong (better than I could paraphrase) or when it is important for my argument that the reader see *exactly* what the author said. *According to Einstein . . .* or *As Shakespeare wrote in* Hamlet . . . or *In her recent address Secretary*

Smith stated. . . . Citing the precise language of respected authorities is strong proof: readers can check your sources and see that, yes, Einstein or Shakespeare or Smith really did write that. Both you and your argument gain strength by association.

Keep in mind that when you write a research paper, it is *your* paper and not that of the experts you cite for support. (Otherwise, you might as well write an introduction and just reprint the sources in their entirety.) In other words, don't just string together many experts in some loose federation hoping their weight alone will make your case.

THE MECHANICS OF DOCUMENTATION

When you use quotations in your paper follow these conventions and you will score high points for clarity.

1. Introduce each quote in your text with a lead that makes it clear who is speaking and why. You advance your case best when the reader knows at all times exactly who is saying what: *According to playwright Arthur Miller* . . . or *On July 10, 1987,* The New York Times *reported.* . . .

2. Quote only as much as you need. In this way, your reader finds all wheat and no chaff and is nourished, not annoyed. I often select a key phrase to establish authority, paraphrasing or summarizing the rest of the author's point:

   In *Fate of the Earth* Jonathan Schell argues that "knowledge is the deterrent" to nuclear war.

3. Use the following punctuation to introduce quotations:
   - Introduce quoted material with a comma. (*According to Jonathan Schell*, "knowledge is the deterrent.") Use the comma unless a colon is called for.
   - Introduce quoted material with a colon if the quotation is an example, a list of items, or explains the previous sentence (see "A Short Guide to Punctuation," Postscript Four, p. 202).

4. Use the following punctuation at the end of quotations:
   - Include commas and periods inside quotation marks. (Fred wondered if knowledge really was "the deterrent.")
   - Put all other punctuation outside the quotation marks. (*What did Schell mean by saying "knowledge is the deterrent"?*) Do so unless the punctuation is part of the

> quoted material itself. (*Fred wondered, "How can knowledge act as a deterrent to war?"*)

- Place footnote numbers outside the quotation marks and outside the end punctuation. (*Knowledge is not, as Schell states, "a deterrent to war."*[1])
- Place parenthetical references outside the quotation marks, but inside the end punctuation. (*Schell argues that "knowledge is a deterrent to war"* (15).)

5. Refer your reader to the source of your quotation in the text itself, in parentheses, following the quote. (The actual mechanics for doing this will be explained at the end of this chapter.)

6. Integrate quotations into your sentence or paragraph in a grammatically correct manner. You have the license to change verb tenses to suit your needs, indicating the substitution by brackets which indicate that you have added text. For example, you can change the past-tense statement, *He was dead last* to its present-tense form, *He [is] dead last* by using brackets. You may also change punctuation and capitalization to suit your sentence needs without noting the change.

7. Indicate omitted words in the middle or at the end of a quoted sentence by using a three-dot ellipsis . . . and omit words at the end of a sentence or whole sentences by an ellipsis plus a period. . . . (This makes four dots in total.) It is not necessary to use an ellipsis to indicate missing words at the beginning of a sentence (*so convention has it. . . .*).

8. If you quote five lines or more, indent the quotation ten spaces, do not surround the indented material with quotation marks—the indentation is the signal that the material is quoted—and type it double space:

> Lead into an indented quotation with a colon. Include author and page number in parentheses at the end of the indented material, after the end punctuation. To be a good example here, I had better write enough sentences to justify an indentation. (Smith 14)

9. Document interviews and site visits appropriately. One of my students did a research report investigating how Ben Cohen and Jerry Greenfield started the local Burlington, Vermont, business that came to be known as "Ben and Jerry's Ice Cream." Here is how he incorporated part of an interview with Jerry Greenfield:

> In order to get the Ben and Jerry's name known, Ben and Jerry started selling the rights to franchise outlets. Jerry explained that "essentially how the franchises work is that someone buys our name, our ice cream, and we do their advertising." (See Appendix A)

In this case, the author included the entire interview as Appendix A and was able to send the reader there for further information.

10. It is often a good idea to evaluate, interpret, or otherwise explain quotations after using them, leaving no doubt in the reader's mind about the point being made. Ignore this advice in cases where the point is obvious.

PARAPHRASE AND SUMMARY

When you repeat another author's ideas in your own words, it is called paraphrase. For example, this passage uses direct quotation: *In* Walden *Henry David Thoreau writes, "Most of the luxuries, and many of the so-called comforts of life, are not only not indispensable, but positive hindrances to the elevation of mankind"* (115). A paraphrase of the same passage might go like this: *In* Walden, *Thoreau argues that material possessions interfere with spiritual thought* (115). (When you cite good writers—especially when you want to look at the literary effect of their language—you may prefer the direct quote, but the paraphrase covers ground a little faster.)

A summary takes even greater liberties than a paraphrase, often trying to condense a great number of pages into a few words. For example, we might summarize Thoreau's entire book this way: Walden *articulates Thoreau's case against materialism in nineteenth-century America.* (In this case, the actual reference to the source is fully included in the sentence itself; if readers want to check the date or publisher of *Walden*, they can turn to the references at the end of your paper.)

In one sense, paraphrase and summary are weaker than direct quotation, because readers realize they are reading material filtered through the author's perspective, not the expert's own formulation. However, paraphrasing saves you space and helps get on with your point more rapidly than direct quotation. I paraphrase when I want to keep the article in my own style; when the material doesn't lend itself to precise quotation; when I want to move quickly; when I want to acknowledge, but not dwell on the idea; and when I know the source well but can't lay my hands on the precise language of the text.

WHO SAID WHAT, WHEN, AND WHERE

If you locate sources of information that help you solve a problem, answer a question, develop a case, or substantiate an idea, you need to tell your readers where you got that information. Who provided it? What did they say? When did they say it? Where can I check it out for myself? The reason you include references, footnotes, and such in research papers is, essentially, to answer those questions.

DIFFERENCES FROM DISCIPLINE TO DISCIPLINE

Each subject area in the curriculum has developed a tradition of documenting sources. Each system does essentially the same thing, but if you are a botany major you'll use the system recommended by the Council of Biology Editors (CBE), while a student of the social sciences will use the American Psychological Association (APA) system, and a student of literature will use the one preferred by the Modern Language Association (MLA). There are other systems, but if you learn something about these three, you will find your way around the others quite easily. If you aren't sure which system to use in writing an academic paper, ask your instructor which he or she prefers; if you want to know which system to use when you write a paper for publication in a professional journal (e.g., *Change, College English*, or *The Journal of Chemical Education*), study the system used in that journal.

The key to documenting your writing well is having access to a style manual that will explain all the principles and show you examples. Most of us know the general principles of documentation, but look up specific items when we need them (for example, how to cite three authors in a two-part article in a popular periodical). I'll explain briefly what is expected in the Name/Title format of documentation and describe how it differs from two other important systems of Name/Date and Number. When you settle on a major, you will want to secure the appropriate style manual expected in your field of study.

The Name/Title System

This system is currently used by writers in English and modern language departments. It came into widespread use in 1984 when the MLA published its latest edition of the *MLA Handbook for Writers of Research Papers*. Until that time, the MLA had recommended the footnote/bibliography system for all documentation. The new MLA practice recommends footnotes or endnotes for only two purposes: (1) for commentary that is not appropriate for the text itself and (2) for multiple sources. (The same rule holds true for such notes in the other documentation formats described here.)

The logic of the MLA format is to keep documentation in your written text brief and simple. You need to include only as much information as your reader needs to locate your complete source at the end of the paper in an alphabetical listing of works cited. Usually the author's name alone, in parentheses, will suffice. Sometimes you need to add the book title, or, if a direct quote, the page number. (In the humanities, the titles of works are held in great reverence and so are considered more important than the dates on which they were published—in the sciences and social sciences, by contrast, the timeliness of research is considered especially important.)

Here are some brief guidelines to help you document correctly in MLA format:

1. When you cite an authority in your text, place his or her last name in parentheses at the end of the sentence making the reference (Twain).
2. When you cite more than one work by an authority, include a shortened version of the title of the book or article after the name in parentheses (Twain, *Huck Finn*).
3. When you include a direct quotation in your citation, include the page number(s) on which the quotation was found:

   > Huck's moral character is evident when he decides not to turn Jim in and exlaims: ''All right then, I'll got to hell!'' (Twain 123).

   Note: After the author's name use neither comma nor ''p.''
4. When you refer to the author of a single work in the text itself, no further documentation is necessary because reference to him or her can be located on the alphabetical ''Works Cited'' page at the end.
5. Keep parenthetical references outside the quotation marks but inside the periods.
6. For works with two authors, use both last names (Smith and Jones). With more than two authors, include only the first author followed by ''et al.'' (Joplin, et al.)
7. At the end of your paper include a ''Works Cited'' page that lists in alphabetical order all the works cited in your paper. Title this page Works Cited.
8. Type all entries double space. Use the following examples to help you cite sources correctly:

SINGLE AUTHOR

Calkins, Lucy McCormick. *Lessons from a Child: On the Teaching and Learning of Writing*. Portsmouth, NH: Heinemann, 1983.

TWO BOOKS BY ONE AUTHOR

Elbow, Peter. *Writing Without Teachers*. New York: Oxford University Press, 1973.
———. *Writing with Power*. New York: Oxford University Press, 1981.

TWO AUTHORS

Strunk, William, Jr., and E. B. White. *The Elements of Style*. 3rd ed. New York: Macmillan, 1979.

MORE THAN TWO AUTHORS

Barr, Mary, et al. *What's Going On? Language/Learning Episodes in British and American Classrooms, Grades 4–13*. Portsmouth, NH: Boynton/Cook, 1982.

ANONYMOUS AUTHOR

American Heritage Dictionary: Second College Edition. Boston: Houghton Mifflin, 1982.

AN EDITOR (OR TWO)

Ellmann, Richard, and Robert O'Clair, eds. *Modern Poems: An Introduction to Poetry*. New York: W. W. Norton, 1976.

MORE THAN TWO VOLUMES

Parrington, Vernon L. *Main Currents in American Thought*, 2 vols. New York: Harcourt, Brace, and World, 1927.

A TRANSLATION

Camus, Albert. *The Stranger*. Trans. Stuart Gilbert. New York: Random House, 1946.

A CHAPTER IN AN ANTHOLOGY

Britton, James. "The Composing Processes and the Functions of Writing." *Research on Composing*. Eds. Charles R. Cooper and Lee Odell. Urbana: National Council of Teachers of English, 1978.

AN UNSIGNED ARTICLE IN A REFERENCE BOOK

"Kiowa Indians." *The Columbia Encyclopedia.* 2nd ed. New York: Columbia University Press, 1956.

AN UNPUBLISHED DISSERTATION

Fulwiler, Toby. "The Failure Story: A Study in American Autobiography." Ph.D. dissertation, The University of Wisconsin, 1973.

A PROFESSIONAL PERIODICAL

Ohmann, Richard. "Reflections on Chaos and Language." *College English 44* (1982): 1–17.

A MONTHLY PERIODICAL

Mayersohn, Norman. "Rad Wheels." *Popular Mechanics* May 1987: 84–87.

DAILY NEWSPAPER

"Ex-Officials See Lobbyists' View." *The Burlington Free Press* 12 April 1987, sec. 2:1.

FILM

The Hustler. Dir. Robert Rossen. With Paul Newman, Jackie Gleason, and George C. Scott, 1961.

RECORD

Springsteen, Bruce. *Nebraska.* Columbia, TC38358, 1982.

TELEVISION/RADIO

Rather, Dan. *CBS Evening News.* 13 April 1991.

PERSONAL INTERVIEW

Strauss, Michael. Telephone interview. Burlington, VT: 12 May 1990.

For more information, consult any edition of the *MLA Handbook* published since 1984. You might also see the *Chicago Manual of Style*, published by the University of Chicago Press, which has complete and lucid explanations of all the major documentation formats.

The Name/Year System

This system is used by most of the social science and professional disciplines, including psychology, sociology, political science, anthropology, education, and business. It is generally referred to as the APA, taking its name from the manual published by the American Psychological Association. The most obvious difference between the MLA and APA is the stress on the date in APA format. When you use this format, keep these principles in mind:

1. When you refer to an author in your text, include date of publication immediately after the name:

   > According to Smith (1986) and Jones (1974) the system is at fault.

2. When you quote directly, but do not mention the author's name in your text, include all necessary information immediately following the quotation: (Smith, 1986, p. 12).
3. When you refer to and quote an author, put date reference immediately following his or her name and page references after the quotation.
4. Title your list of sources at the paper's end "References."
5. On your reference page, include the date immediately after the author, capitalize only the first major word in the title, and include "p." or "pp." for page numbers.

   > Dawkins, Richard (1987). *The Blind watchmaker*. New York: Norton.

6. Include a separate title page for the paper.
7. Write a 50- to 75-word abstract and place it immediately after the title page.

(This is a necessarily brief discussion of how APA differs from MLA. If you are required to work regularly in this system, consult the *Publication Manual of the American Psychological Association* or Kate Turabian's *A Manual for Writers of Term Papers, Theses, and Dissertations*, published by the University of Chicago Press.)

The Name/Year system is also used by the life sciences, including biology, botany, genetics, physiology, and zoology. This CBE system varies in small ways from the APA system. For example, book and journal titles are *not* underlined on the reference page in CBE; they are in APA. (For more information on the Name/Year system as used in the life sciences, consult the *CBE Style Manual*, published by the Council of Biology Editors.)

The Number System

This method of documentation is used in the quantitative and physical sciences such as chemistry, computer science, mathematics, and physics. Each field has its own distinct variation of this system, so you will need to consult one of the specialized reference works listed below for details. Look briefly at the system used in many computer science journals as an example.

In computer science, you are required to compile a list of the cited works, in the order they appear in the paper, not in alphabetical order:

> 1. Franklin, P. . . .
> 2. Smith, R. . . .
> 3. Miller, J. . . .
> 4. Jones, M. and J. Wesson . . .

Each time you refer to that source, include the corresponding number in parentheses (2) or raised superscript[3] in your text:

> It has been established by Smith (2) and Miller (3) that ice cream melts at 33 degrees. Others (1,4), however, claim it melts at 32 degrees.

For more information on Number System documentation consult the following sources:

> 1. Chemistry. *Handbook for Authors of Papers in American Chemical Society Publications.*
> 2. Mathematics. *A Manual for Authors of Mathematical Papers*, published by the American Mathematical Society.
> 3. Physics. *Style Manual for Guidance in the Preparation of Papers*, published by the American Institute of Physics.

This chapter outlines general guidelines for documentation. If you follow them you will not go far astray. It is always safest to consult your instructor directly to see what system he or she wishes you to employ.

SUGGESTIONS FOR JOURNAL WRITING

1. What documentation system will you need to know for your intended major? Have you used it yet? Take a few minutes and see if you can write out from memory its major features.

2. After reading this chapter, what questions do you still have about using documentation correctly in your writing?

SUGGESTIONS FOR RESEARCH ESSAYS

1. **INDIVIDUAL:** Search the library for periodicals important to your intended major or field of study and take notes on the documentation forms you find there. Learn the system and make sure you use it in your next discipline-specific paper.

2. **COLLABORATIVE:** With other similar majors in this class, write a Guide to Documentation appropriate for first-year college students, being sure to write it in a language they easily understand.

Chapter 18

FINDING YOUR VOICE

> If you feel that you can never write as well as John Steinbeck [or]
> Charles Dickens . . . you may be right. But you can write well . . . if
> you find a voice that rings true to you and you learn to record the
> surprises of the world faithfully.
>
> Ken Macrorie, *Telling Writing*. Portsmouth, NH: Hayden, 1976.

Early in this book, we looked at the several purposes that cause
people to write in the first place: to learn something better, to question, to share, and to present. Later, we looked at the audiences for
whom writers write, including teachers, friends, the public, and
oneself. In this final chapter, I'd like to reflect on the writer's "voice"
and to consider how it develops.

In a book such as this, a discussion of voice in writing belongs
either first, because it's so important, or last, because it's so slippery. I
have saved it for last because, ultimately, voice is something that
develops unconsciously or intuitively and largely apart from the
more conscious techniques we have studied.

The concept that each speaker or writer has a unique voice, one
that's indisputably his or hers, is perhaps the most difficult idea in this
book. I'd like to think that with each sentence and paragraph in these
chapters you can hear *me* speaking—that you can imagine the same
person speaking, page after page, without ever having met the author.
I'd like to think you can, for that is the best illustration of voice that I
can think of, but I cannot judge how you hear me.

But what really constitutes a writer's voice? The type and length
of words, sentences, and paragraphs? The ideas expressed in the

paragraphs? The arrangement of the ideas into a whole? The values embedded in the ideas? Some unidentifiable quality best described as mystical? Or, as some would argue, do we each have many voices, which vary according to one's purpose and audience? It will be the business of this chapter to explore where voice lies and what control, if any, writers have over it.

THE STYLE OF VOICE

Think a little bit about Cicero's definition of rhetoric: "The good man speaking well." (Changed to nonsexist language—"the good person speaking well"—the rhythm is less, but the content is more.) What I enjoy about this simple definition is the implied attention to the character of the whole speaker: What he or she stands for. What he or she believes. The quality of his or her words. The truth of those words. And the embedded notion that these words are, in fact, his or her own.

When we consider written instead of oral speech, the concept of voice becomes even more difficult to pin down. In writing, we can't, of course, hear the timbre of the voice or see the expressions on the face. Instead, we hear the voice through our reading, perhaps gleaning our first clues about the writer from the particular combination of words, punctuation, sentences, and paragraphs that we call *style*.

If I look for a moment at my own style, as evidenced in this chapter, a few things become obvious:

1. I use lots of first-person pronouns ("I") to let you know that these are *my* truths, not somebody else's. Other books about college writing assert things quite different from those found here.
2. I frequently use contractions to make my voice more conversational and less formal. In fact, I'd like this book to read like conversations between you and me about writing, only I have to imagine your concerns and questions.
3. As much as possible, I eschew large or pretentious words (like *eschew*, which simply means "avoid") because that's how I speak with my family, friends, and students.
4. And I use a fair number of qualifiers (*fair*, *well*, *rather*, *perhaps*, *of course*). I want to suggest that my assertions are not absolute, to give the reader time to chew on the assertions, and to help readers hear the tone of my informal speaking voice.

Of course, there are more observations we could make about my style—about clause length, fragments, figures of speech, active versus passive verbs, punctuation patterns, sentence rhythms, and the like, but this will do. Style is a matter of choices—some conscious and some not—about the language impression you leave behind.

To the extent that we control our style, we control our voice. We modify our language—sometimes consciously, sometimes not—to suit our several purposes and audiences. Especially at the editing stage, after we have worked out our central ideas, we have the luxury of going back over our draft and selecting just the right word or phrase to convey an idea: to select the word "large" rather than "big," "huge," "enormous," or "humongous." At this level of construction, we choose words to represent our ideas in one way rather than in another. But we don't have time to edit everything that comes out, nor do we want to, and so we probably make more unconscious than conscious choices.

THE CONTENT OF VOICE

The voice you find in a piece of writing is much more than a matter of style; otherwise, this chapter would be nearly over. When someone reads my writing and tells me that they could hear my *voice*, I take that as different from telling me they liked my style. "Voice" implies for me a deeper, more permanent resonance; *style* implies surface elements that are readily manipulated to produce various effects.

In addition to style, there is something that I stand for, some set of beliefs and ideas that characterize me as distinct from you—that, too, is a part of voice. There are some sentences that I could not utter, so foreign are they to my particular way of thinking and living. (At least I'd like to think that's true.) I'd like to think that the words of a Hitler, Stalin, a Ku Klux Klansman, or a terrorist could not appear among my utterances, nor those of the beer commercials on television, nor those of some colleagues down the hall. *My* voice not only permeates my words, but reflects my thoughts and values as well.

THE ARRANGEMENT OF VOICE

My voice also arranges, organizes, and focuses whatever material comes before it. In other words, voice is also a matter of the patterns through which we see and express the world. From even this chapter you will see the degree to which I am governed by logic or emotion, am inductive rather than deductive, am linear or circular, am probing or casual. Do I begin a piece of writing with an anecdote or a proposition? Do I provide examples for all of my generalizations?

Arranging ideas is easier in writing than in speaking because we can see our thoughts. In writing, we have the leisure to develop a thought carefully, to work from an outline, and to review and revise until we are satisfied that the order of presentation is as strong as we can make it.

THE EVOLUTION OF VOICE

Ultimately, when we communicate in writing, *style*, *content*, and *arrangement* are all working together simultaneously, somehow combining to represent us. Although we modify elements of our voices from time to time, person to person, situation to situation, we are more likely to play variations on a theme than to make radical departures from some fundamental expression that has come to represent us. Yes, I can write like an impartial, dispassionate, passive-voiced scientist if called upon to do so. Yes, I can write free-association, stream-of-consciousness mind play if I'm in certain moods. But these are not the me you'll usually find when you read what I write most often: my journal, letters, memos, articles, and books.

Your voice is something you may create consciously as you do a research paper or a poem. But more often it's what spills out whenever you talk candidly to your friends and when you write in your journal or to your mother, a classmate, or a teacher. Your voice evolves over time as you do. What I write today is basically the same as I would have written five years ago, but a little different, because I'm a little different at 48 than I was at 38 or 28 or 18. You are who you are, and when you speak or write it is reasonable to expect that your language represents you—if not your language, what does?

HOW MANY VOICES?

I *do* have more than one voice. I *can* become other people when I choose. I am even capable (sometimes) of uttering thoughts in which I do not believe. In short, whenever I write, to some extent I am putting on an act, the meaning of which changes as my purpose does. In this view, each of us is also a collection of several voices, none more genuine than another.

Whether we each believe we have one or many voices may simply depend upon how we define the word *voice*. When I asked the students in my advanced writing class how many voices they had, their answers differed in interesting ways. For example, Jen insisted that she had only one:

My voice always maintains, if not screeches, an egocentric notion of who I am.

Carter insisted that all writers have only one:

Good writers or bad, we cannot change our voice from one moment to the next. We can disguise it with style, but our own voices will ring true.

However, Bobby and Lisa both believed they each had three distinct voices, though each described these differently:

BOBBY: I think I have three different writing voices: one academic, one personal, and one which lies somewhere in between. The ones I use most are the two extremes.

LISA: I have three voices: the first is a writing-for-the-teacher voice, the second is a letter-writing voice, the last is a train-of-thought voice. . . . I am more comfortable with the last two— they are both like a real person speaking.

And Kim believed she had many:

the writing home voice, the chemistry-lab voice, the writing-to-boyfriend voice, the writing-to-best-friend voice, the freshman English voice, the journal voice. Each one requires me to author it, but my actual presence in the piece will be stronger or lighter depending on the topic.

What may be most important in this discussion is not whether you actually have one, three, six, or more voices, but your awareness that your readers hear one whether you like it or not.

To first-year college writers, I usually put it this way: We each have some bundle of beliefs, values, and behaviors that constitutes who we are (including our own perception of who we are). When we write, we represent some part of that self-concept on paper. Unless, for certain purposes, we choose to modify it—at which time the shape of our voice becomes more problematic, less clearly *us*, more possibly some single quality exaggerated: the scientific me, the poetic me.

As a writer, you will be most versatile to the extent that you can assume a variety of voices, some less comfortable than others, perhaps, but possible. Learn, then, to view your voice as a powerful personal tool that you can shape as the occasion demands, recognizing that some shapes can become gross distortions of that for which you generally stand.

HEARING THE VOICE

In one of my freshman writing classes, Stephany chose to write about her summer job on an egg farm. I watched her write several drafts, her voice getting stronger and more assertive as she wrote. If we look at the first paragraphs of three of her drafts, we will see Stephany's voice in various stages of development.

Draft One: This last summer my father said I had to get a job. I got a job
9/6   at a girls' camp, but I didn't dig the idea and hoped that
             something better would come up. Much to my distaste, I ap-
             plied for a job at a nearby egg farm. I wasn't all that thrilled
             with the prospects of spending the summer picking eggs, but
             it would mean more money, so I said "what the hell" and ap-
             plied.

Stephany moves in this opening paragraph from her father to the girls' camp to the egg farm in a rambling, informal adolescent voice. Yes, I hear someone talking—complaining, actually—but despite the profanity, I do not find Stephany's voice to be especially distinctive here: she tells us what she doesn't like, but nothing of what she does.

In her next draft, Stephany concentrated on the job at the egg farm from her opening and dropped the indecisive period leading up to it.

Draft Two: My summer job was at Arnold's Egg Farms in Lakeview,
9/7   Maine. I was the candler for Complex 70's, a series of ten
             barns. I worked six days a week, Thursday through Tuesday.

Here Stephany has the tight focus, but has lost most of the verbal cues that told us something about her personality. I would describe the voice here as fairly objective and cautious, with no boldly distinctive qualities to make us know much of the writer herself.

Her last draft started like this:

Draft Three: T.G.I.T. Thank God It's Tuesday. I always look forward to
9/16   Tuesdays. They mean two things: Tomorrow is my day off
              and today is my boss's day off, so I won't be asked to pick
              eggs. I really hate picking eggs—I get all covered with dust,
              eggs, and grain. By the end of the day, I'm so tired that I
              just want to sack out. When I was hired, my boss told me
              I'd only have to pick eggs once in a while, but this week I
              had to pick three times. It really gets me, because my real
              job is candling eggs.

Stephany has changed more than her style here: she now starts fast, with a little riddle; she includes good details; she writes with new rhythm. But I would argue that the real gain in this draft is in the totality of her voice. In place of an aimless, complaining teenager or a technical report writer, we find a whole, self-assertive, mildly cocky, genuinely humorous person. After she found the story she really wanted to tell, her voice got stronger and her overall writing much better.

FINDING YOUR VOICE

It's an interesting exercise to try to discover the origins and nature of your own voice. In the last assignment of the semester, I asked my first-year writing students to do just that—to reconstruct, by examining past writing, how their writing voices developed, and to locate the features that presently characterize them. Some students, such as Amy, went all the way back to their elementary school writing:

> One of the earliest things I can remember writing is a story called "Bill and Frank." It was about a hot dog (Frank) who could sing and play the banjo. Bill was the hot dog vendor who discovered his talent and became his manager. I wrote this story somewhere around third grade. It was very short, simple and to the point.
>
> As the school years passed, assignments got more and more complex. Short, simple and to the point was no longer a plausible style. Of course, page requirements often went along with these assignments also causing a change in style.

She also remembered major influences on the developoment of her voice:

> My first taste of truly more complex writing was in my ninth grade European history class. Mr. Page taught me how to write an essay. He taught me about making a thesis, supporting this thesis with evidence (from documented sources), and writing a conclusion.

Other students found truly negative influences on their development as writers. Here Steve remembers Mr. Higgins with some anger:

> Mr. Higgins was always on our case about grammar. I don't blame him for it, but he taught it totally wrong. He forced it upon you. It is harder when you have to learn all those picky rules all at

once. I think you can learn much easier by just plain writing. The more you write the more you use words. By the continuous use of sentences the learning becomes natural.

And Karen remembers not so much a single influence as her own attitude towards writing, which was well developed by the time she was a high school senior:

> As I look back and review my writing habits I discover a pattern: name, date, title, one draft, spell check, done!! I handed it in and never looked at it again. My senior thesis, I sat down at the computer, typed out a draft, and as soon as the page numbers reached ten I wrote a conclusion, ran it through spell check, and handed it in. I never proofread it. I was content it didn't have any spelling errors. So, why did I get a "D" on it? I couldn't figure it out.

In completing this assignment to analyze their own writing voices, many college writers reported a new awareness of themselves as writers, of their voices as distinctly their own. Colleen, for example, for the first time believes she is a writer:

> The important part of my growth as a writer is the fact that I have grown into a writer rather than grown as a writer. I never used to consider myself a writer and perhaps now I am being too bold by saying that I have become one. I used to be afraid of writing. I despised anything that resembled a diary. It was hard for me to get the idea into my head that writing was for your personal use. That's what I think writing is all about.

Gavin reports major growth in selecting certain topics:

> My major development as a writer has occurred in the topics that I write on. Through the years I have focused on continually more powerful subjects. From violence in children's literature to the destruction of tropical rain forests to gang violence to my work this year on nursing homes and the homeless.

While Wendy views her changes as a writer as closely akin to her changes as a person:

> Changing one's personal voice is sort of like changing one's personality . . . I see that as I grew older, my writing matured,

became more open, and developed in the same ways I did as a person.

Anthony took a different approach to this assignment and looked only at the writing he had done since our course began. Here is what he found:

> I want my reader to be enthusiastic about reading my paper. I want to be able to say proudly, "I wrote this and it ain't that bad."
> My first essay was telling the story instead of showing it. Here's a small clip.
>
>> The great thing about baseball is that it's always throwing a different pitch at you, one has to expect the unexpected. . . . . It's hard to express in writing the feelings these teams can give you.
>
> The language in the above paragraph is acceptable, but it's not conveying the feelings I had. After three pages of that even I get a little tired with it after reading it a couple of times. I'm giving the reader an evaluation of what I thought, not letting them come to their own evaluations by giving them the reason for mine. In the next example, a later draft of the same essay shows my attempt at showing not telling.
>
>> BANG . . . It was going, heading straight for the upperdeck in right field, the home crowd stood but was silent.
>
> The feeling is more evident in the writing the reader can witness it too. Just having me tell you how I feel alone is not enough but to let you feel the same is more powerful writing. This is one of the major changes in my writing style from 4 months ago to now.

DEVELOPING YOUR WRITING VOICE

Voice is difficult to isolate and analyze. I've chosen to write about it last because your voice to a large extent is determined by your other skills and beliefs. However, there are some things you can do that will have a positive impact on your writing voice. None will be as important as living, learning, working, loving, raising families, and growing older, but each will help the process along.

1. Speak when you are afraid. You grow fastest when you take the most risks, slowest when you remain safe. For me as an undergraduate, speaking out loud in class was as risky as anything I had ever done, but until I tested my voice and my beliefs in the arena of the class, I really didn't know who I

was, what I stood for, or what I *could* stand for. The more you test your oral voice, literally, the more your written voice will develop.

2. Keep a log or journal. These are safer places in which to take risks than classrooms, so take advantage of that as often as you can. The more you explore who you are in your journal, the more easily you will be able to assert that identity both out loud and in your more formal writing. Use your journal to rehearse your public self.

3. Share your writing with others. Sharing is another form of risk taking, of being willing to see how others perceive you. Asking friends, roommates, classmates, and teachers to respond to your writing in general, to your voice in particular, helps you see how your voice affects others, which in turn allows you to tinker with it for this or that effect. If you hear good things back about your writing, you will be most likely to do more writing; if you hear bad things, you won't write. Pick your sharing audience carefully!

4. Notice other people's voices. One of the best means of growing in every direction at once is simply reading. The more you read, the more other voices you learn about. Read and notice how others convey this or that impression. Take reading notes in your journal to capture what you found. Notice the writers who make you keep reading and notice those who put you to sleep, and try to determine why.

5. Practice other people's voices. One of the best of the old-fashioned composition exercises was copying, word for word, the style of someone else. One day you copy a passage from Virginia Woolf, the next day you try Thomas Wolfe, then Tom Wolfe, then you try to determine which is which and why. These exercises also help you notice what features characterize your own writing.

OBSERVATION

As I've presented it here, the matter of voice is fairly complex. I've suggested that, on the one hand, we each have a voice that is ours; yet I've also suggested that we have more than one voice. I've also suggested that voice is something that develops over time—over one's lifetime, actually—but I've also shown a sample of voice developing itself over a several-week draft. As I said at the outset, the concept of voice is both important and slippery: others perceive us as our language represents us. Some of this we don't control, at least not yet, and some we never will.

SUGGESTIONS FOR JOURNAL WRITING

1. Explain your understanding of voice in writing. How would you describe your own?

2. What influences have determined your current writing voice(s)? That is, can you think of particular teachers or a parent or an incident that influenced how you write today?

3. Describe how you vary or change your voice according to whom you are writing to.

SUGGESTIONS FOR ESSAY WRITING

1. Write an analysis of your current writing voice. Collect as much of your recent (during the past year) writing as you can in a single folder. Consider writing you did in previous schools (for example, high school if that was recent), in other college courses, earlier in this course, copies of letters, personal diaries, or journals. Arrange these samples one of several ways: for example, according to subject, type, audience. Then examine each specimen and identify the features that seem to characterize your own voice—those that appear from piece to piece: style? attitude? arrangement? word choice? subject? Write a report describing that voice, using your analyzed data as evidence. (You could report the results of this study in either first or third person—try a passage of each to appreciate the difference.)

2. Describe the development of your current writing voice. Follow the procedures described above, but go back as far as you are able (middle school? elementary school?) and arrange your samples chronologically. Look from sample to sample and see if you can determine any pattern or see any evolution in the development of this voice. Write an essay describing and speculating about your personal evolution as a writer, using both samples and memories of particular influences to help you.

SUGGESTIONS FOR RESEARCH WRITING

1. **INDIVIDUAL:** Research the concept of voice in the library. Start with authors such as Irving Goffman, Walker Gibson, and Loren Eiseley. Write a paper in which you examine the degree to which a writer's voices are determined by particular social influences (neighborhood, school, religion, family, friends, etc.) acting upon them.

2. **COLLABORATIVE:**   Write a voice profile. Pair up with somebody else. Interview each other about the nature of your writing
   and speaking voices. In addition, you might ask to see samples of
   each other's writing. Write a profile describing each other's
   voices, using interview and written material as data to support
   you. Conclude each report with a response by the person interviewed: How accurately have you portrayed his or her voice?

Postscript One

WRITING WITH COMPUTERS

What I have to say about computers actually begins with myself, for they have changed my professional life in powerful and positive ways. They have, in fact, been the most significant influence on my own writing during the twenty-odd years that I have been making a living as a teacher and writer.

However, you must understand at the outset that I approach computers as a writer, not a whiz. I don't have the faintest idea of how my aging IBM PC works or how to program, upgrade, accelerate, turbocharge, or otherwise modify it. I have learned only as much of WordStar as I need to get the immediate jobs done: I still don't know how to footnote, index, mail-merge, or get my thesaurus to find the synonyms that my manual tells me are in the box. I have failed to learn any word-processing programs other than WordStar—even allegedly easier or better ones—though I have twice tried. And I am such a lousy typist that I have permanently glued an elevated wooden extension (sanded smooth, varnished, and nice looking) onto my delete key so that I can hit it every word or two with a deft backhand and so avoid hitting, by mistake, the insert key next to it.

In other words, my credentials for writing authoritatively about the role of computers in writing programs seem a little slim—some might even say suspect. However, I will argue that their very slimness actually makes what credentials I have quite useful.

COMPUTERS FOR THE WRITER

I would like to observe closely what I have learned myself during the last nine years writing with a word processor, hoping that these personal lessons may provide answers to the questions with which this appendix begins.

1. **Computers are easy and forgiving typewriters.** They make it possible for even mediocre typists to enjoy the substantial benefits of seeing our language represented in uniform typescript immediately and correctly before our eyes. Our writing looks nicer typed, which is a plus should anyone else happen to read it, but more importantly for us as writers, it looks farther away, almost as if someone else had produced it and not our own hand. Therefore, we see the shape and substance of our expressions more quickly and clearly, which allows us to determine what else, if anything, we wish to do with them before we make them public.

2. **Computers are remarkably complete writing systems.** Even inexpensive word-processing programs now include comprehensive resource programs, including dictionaries and thesauruses in addition to invention, editing, and formatting guides. Spell-checkers may be the most commonly used supplement for writers, useful for many of us as proofreaders—fast, though not foolproof. As a writer I can always use a quick proofread, knowing that when I proof unaided I'm likely to read right through my own typos and misspellings. However, speaking as a writer, I know that I trust my own ear on matters of grammar and style—which I think is the case for most native speakers of English. (Neither I nor anyone I know uses programs that purport to analyze style, grammar, and punctuation; however, my very ignorance of such programs may be a telling comment on their ultimate usefulness to experienced writers.)

3. **Computers are wonderful editing machines.** They allow me to do an infinite amount of tinkering to get words precise and sentences just right. The distance provided by the typescript helps here, but the electronic impermanence is even more important, as insert and delete keys make all of my expressions instantly modifiable, allowing me to view first one construction, then another, in quick succession.

4. **Computers rapidly format my thought and language.** They make it possible for all of us, from poets to technical report writers, to play with lines, space, margins, and blocks of text until the effect is pleasing and clear. In addition, of course, computers combined with laser printers make desktop publishing easy and fairly inexpensive. I know this not

from my own experience but from my students' and other writers' well-made works.

5. **Computers make information retrieval and transfer easy.** Again, though I have yet to purchase a modem, which allows for the easy and accurate transfer of text over telephone lines, I have used our library's on-line catalogue system often enough to recognize its utility. A modem at home would give me direct and rapid access to near and distant knowledge, and to collaborating easily with co-writers on long-distance writing projects. Electronic mail is already making life easier for several friends of mine; this too I will soon learn.

6. **Computers are the ultimate revision machines.** I value most the immediate chance provided by seeing my thoughts objectified on a screen because that means I can re-see, review, and re-cast them until they please me and represent me well. While the insert and delete keys are crucial here, as they are in editing, the greatest advantage is the capability to mark and move blocks of text within and between files. On the computer I can no longer count the separate acts of revision—they take place simultaneously with the generation of new text. Because I revise more easily—hence more often—I am sure that computers have made my finished drafts thematically more coherent and stylistically more polished. (They have not, as once I imagined, helped me to write *more* or *faster*, but I am convinced they help me to write *better*.)

7. **Finally, computers are idea machines.** Computers actually affect the nature, shape, texture, and quality of my thought—though I can't prove this. Before computers, I used to generate several pages—sometimes several dozen pages—in linear sequence, one after another, on yellow pads in pencil, seldom revising or editing along the way. With computers, I'm more likely to generate no more than a single paragraph before I begin developing, illustrating, deleting, changing, extending, finding new implications for it—only then moving on to my second paragraph. In fact, the second paragraph will usually spring from the middle—not the end—of the first with a touch of the return key. In other words, computers actually cause me to write from the inside out, subdividing my paragraphs amoeba-like, with the third paragraph often springing from the middle of the second, and so on.

What all this means for you is simply this: get your hands on a computer as soon as you are able, learn to type (programs to teach you to type are available for your computer), and begin to do all of your college-level writing in this and other courses with your computer. I believe that if you learn to use this machine—whatever it is, IBM, Apple, Brand X—and whatever your word processing program—WordStar, Macwrite, Brand X—your writing should improve, along with your grades. Here are some suggestions that may help you as a computer writer:

1. Learn to compose directly on your computer. Get in the habit of writing and revising on screen; it will save you from using the computer as a glorified typewriter. I still do journal writing longhand, and I make revision comments to myself by hand on printed out copy. But when I know I'm writing formally, for publication, I get to a computer as soon as I can and start—anywhere—to get language on the screen and let that language help develop my thought further.

2. Experiment with the suggestions in the chapter "JOURNALS: HOW TO," but do them on the computer. While I don't keep a computer journal, I know several people who do and who prefer that mode to handwriting in a small notebook.

3. Try the various ideas in the chapter "COMPOSING: HOW TO," but do them on your computer. All the composing processes, from *drafting* to *revising* to *editing*, are easier, faster, and more satisfying with a good word-processing system on your computer.

4. Back up everything. No excuses here. Before you turn off your machine, make one extra copy on a separate disk, whether you use floppies or a hard disk makes no difference, they can all go bad (and they have for me). Your teachers use computers and know about backing up files and probably have very little patience with the "bad disk" excuse.

5. Make a new file for every draft you write. First make a back-up file on the same disk (most computers do this automatically when you save a file); then rename it [*Paper title*].2 and make changes on it; when you change a draft again, make a back-up and name it [*Paper Title*].3, and so on. This way you can retrieve early drafts any time you wish, which should give you the confidence to take great liberties in revising the paper.

6. Take great liberties with each new draft. Try new leads, new structures, new forms and see what they look like. That's how a lot of good writing gets done—with the writer experimenting to see how things might look this way instead of that. It's not the same doing it only in your head. And since you've made back-up disk copies and back-up files (on the same disk), you know you can always go back to the old one if what you try does not work out.

7. Try sharing disks directly with classmates for feedback. This is especially helpful with collaborative projects, but may be useful on individual ones as well. Write to the other writers directly on their disks, using all capital letters or brackets or italics to differentiate your comments from their text. This mode of response gives the writer the ideas—sometimes rather extensive ones—right in the text where they are most useful.

8. Use a spell-checker, but don't trust it. At least not entirely. It catches typos and spelling errors—but only if the mistake isn't itself also a word: if you mis-type ''of'' instead of ''if'' the program won't flag it. Some catch repeated words, some don't. Learn the limits of your particular program and it will help you a lot, since most of us are our own worst proofreaders. But proofread also by hand, moving a ruler slowly down the page, reading again each word as you go. (I *always* find one more mistake when I do this.)

9. Locate and use a reliable printer with a good ribbon. If you own a printer there's no excuse for not changing your ribbon often enough to make good clear dark copies. This is especially important in classes that ask you to make multiple copies for distribution. If you need to go to another place to print—the library or a friend—don't wait until ten minutes before class to do so: There may be a line or a malfunction and then you're stuck. (I'm as tired of the ''broken printer'' excuse as I am of the ''bad disk'' excuse.) Remember, too, that photocopy machines make multiple copies much faster than public printers, so if people are lined up behind you to print, make one copy and the rest photocopies.

10. Make perfect final copy. There's no excuse any more for sloppy looking papers. Computers let you revise until your product is perfect. And good printers make your words look even more profound than they really are. If you don't take care here, on your final draft, your classmates will, and your work may suffer by comparison.

Postscript Two

GUIDELINES FOR WRITING GROUPS

Writing gets better by reading, practice, and response. The first two you can do for yourself by selecting books that stimulate your interest and show you interesting prose styles, and by writing regularly in a journal or on a computer and not settling for drafts that don't please you. But at some point, to get really better, you need to hear other people respond to your words and ideas. If you are using this book in a class, chances are that your teacher confers with you individually about your work, and chances are that you meet every week or so with your classmates in a writing group where you take turns receiving and giving responses. During the last several years my students and I worked together to develop guidelines to help writing groups work even more smoothly.

TO THE CLASS

1. Writing groups work best in classrooms where there is a sense of community and trust. All members of a given class share the responsibility for making this happen.
2. Permanent writing groups of four to six work best in most classes. Fewer than four makes a weaker dynamic—though two's and three's are fast and work well for ad hoc situations where you have only fifteen or twenty minutes. More than six becomes cumbersome for time and equal participation—though larger groups work very well outside of class where time is less restricted. So I shoot for groups of about five and plan for these to stay together for the duration of a given

assignment, meeting preferably once a week for a series of weeks. For new assignments, I suggest forming new groups.

3. The length of a given paper determines what happens to it in a group. It's possible for four or five papers of four or five pages to be read and commented on in their entirety in a fifty-minute class. With longer papers, writers need to read selections from their paper or take turns being featured. (I use a rule of thumb that it takes two minutes to read a page of typed double-spaced writing.)

4. It's helpful to distribute papers before class so that readers have had a chance to make private comments. However, in most classrooms, early distribution is very difficult. The following suggestions are made on the assumption that people show up in class with fresh papers to be talked about.

5. Groups work best when they become habit. Keep the groups meeting regularly and keep the group meeting time sacred. Jettison other things before you jettison group time in class. What does the teacher do while you all meet in groups? I stay out of all groups for the first few meetings, then participate in a group if invited.

TO THE WRITER

1. Plan to read your paper *out loud* to the others in your group. Hearing a paper read by the author adds a special dimension to the writing—for the reader as well as the listening audience. There's no substitute for a little rehearsal reading aloud before class—you'll be surprised at how much you notice yourself, both positive and negative, about your writing when you hear yourself read it.

2. Prepare enough copies of your paper for each person in the group. If finances are short, two could look at one copy together, following you while you read aloud. Without duplicate copies it's difficult for your audience to remember all the language they would like to comment on. (If you cannot make extra copies, plan to read your paper—or portions of it—out loud twice.)

3. Direct your listeners' response: Sometimes ask for general reactions: "How does it sound?" "Is it believable?" "What do you like best?" "Where does it need more work?" "What questions do you have?" "What do you expect next?"

4. Sometimes ask for more focused responses about the parts of the paper that you most want to hear about: "Does my

introduction work? Why?" "Which evidence for my argument is most convincing?" "How would you describe my tone?" "Am I too colloquial? too formal? inconsistent?" "Does my conclusion conclude?" "Does it sound like me talking?" (You will notice that you get more mileage if you are able to phrase questions that can't simply be answered "Yes" or "No.")

5. Sometimes ask for assignment-specific responses: "Where is my interpretation most convincing?" "What holes do you see in my analysis?" "Where do you think I 'show' versus 'summarize'?" "Does effect clearly follow cause? If not, why not?" "What details tell you that I was really there?"

6. Try some response exercises, such as those Peter Elbow describes in *Writing with Power* (Oxford, 1981): Ask people to tell you the "movies of their mind" as they listened to you—what impressions the language created, emotional or otherwise, as you read. Or ask for metaphors stimulated by the writing. Or ask them to summarize your paper back to you. Each of these exercises gives you a different kind of information to help you rewrite.

7. Listen more than talk. The writing group is your chance to hear others' reactions unaided by your own biases. Listen to your groupmates, say as little as possible, and try not to get defensive. Instead, take good notes and plan to use your verbal energy revising for next time. (It's very nice to hear nice things about your work and very hard to hear criticism, but both are very instructive.)

8. Keep track of time or have a timekeeper do so for you. You each want your fair share and it's a good idea to allocate it evenly at the start: If you've got five papers in fifty minutes, stick pretty close to ten minutes apiece.

9. At the end of your time, collect copies from people who have written responses to you and say some kind of thank you.

10. It's your paper. Revise based on your own best judgment, not necessarily what the group told you. This is especially true if you hear contradictory responses. But to ignore the group suggestions altogether may also be a mistake, especially if you find more than one group member making the same comment. And remember that if you have a chance to read to the same group again, they will be especially attuned to whether or not you took any of their suggestions.

TO THE AUDIENCE

1. Look for what the writer asks. Follow along silently as the paper is read and try to focus on the kind of response the writer wants, at least at first.

2. Mark small things such as typos and errors in spelling or punctuation, but do not spend group time on such comments. Plan to return your copy to the writer at the end of the session with such items marked or corrected, preferably in pencil, never in red ink.

3. Say something nice about the writer's work. In spite of the value of critical comments, we grow as much by comments which confirm that we are doing something right. People are much more willing to listen to critical comments once they feel confident that much of their work is good.

4. Ask questions. If you find problems with the paper, the most effective comment is often a question to the writer about the spot or intent or language or format or whatever: "What did you mean here?" "What would happen if you told this story in the present tense?" "What were some examples that might support you here?" Questions point to problems but do not dictate solutions.

5. Share emotional as well as intellectual responses. Sometimes it's good for a writer simply to know how you felt about something.

6. Be specific. Try to identify the word, sentence, paragraph, page where you had this or that response. That way a writer has something concrete to react to.

7. Don't overwhelm the writer by commenting on absolutely everything you found bothersome about her paper. Try to mention the most important issues out loud in the group and let others go.

8. Share your response time equitably among group members. One good way to do this is for each of you in turn to say one quick thing, asking the writer to remain quiet while you do. This guarantees that you all participate at some level. The discussion will naturally go on from there.

9. Be honest. If you really find nothing you like, don't invent things that are not true. But in twenty-three years of teaching, I've never found a paper about which something positive could not be said (and I don't mean inane things such as "Nice spelling!" or "Deft use of commas"). So maybe the best advice here is "be honest, gently."

10. Stick to the paper. While it's fun and sometimes fruitful to digress into related but peripheral issues, keep in mind that your time—if you're critiquing in class—is brief. And keep your comments focused on the writing, not the writer— that helps keep egos and personalities out of the work at hand, which is writing good papers.

Postscript Three

ADVICE TO POOR SPELLERS

There's no magic in this appendix, just common sense for people who find themselves, at the end of their secondary education, to be poor spellers. I'm not sure why some people take more readily to spelling than others, but it's a small problem that writers have to wrestle with as they ply their craft.

What you need to know is that accurate spelling has little to do with good writing. Yes, good writing no doubt includes properly spelled words, but there's no telling how they got that way: in the first draft? using a spell-checker on the final draft? by having a good editor?

A piece of writing says exactly the same thing whether or not it contains spelling errors. Be clear about that. Misspelling is seldom a matter of meaning: The reason the spelling offends is that the reader knows how the word is supposed to be spelled in the first place. Spelling is a matter of manners more than meaning. To submit your writing to someone else, be it a parent, teacher, boss, or friend, with misspelled words sends a message about you as a person and leads your audience to make certain inferences, none of them pleasant or necessarily accurate: that you are not well educated, that you don't read, that you are not a careful person, that you are not intelligent. Not fair, you say? I agree, but that's the way the culture works.

Following are some strategies to help you cope with, though not solve, your ailment.

1. Decide that spelling is important. If you do this, you'll take the first and most necessary step to becoming a better

speller: You'll become aware that you do occasionally—or frequently—spell words incorrectly. (I'm in the occasional group myself.)

2. Write with a computer and get a word-processing program with a good spell-checker. The easiest and most reliable help for poor spellers is to get in the habit of putting all drafts through this program. You'll still have to look up most proper names and it won't catch mistakes that result in other words (typing "do" for "to" or "right" for "write"), but it will catch a lot.

3. In addition to or instead of a computer, find a friend whom you trust and ask for quick spell-checking before you call your draft finished. You might offer to check his or her draft in exchange: All of us recognize more misspellings than we know how to correct ourselves.

4. Begin keeping a list of words you misspell most often. Do this in your notebook or journal, and pay some regular attention to them—can you learn them now?

5. Notice the words you most often misspell and see if you can think of a trick to tell you the correct way. I learned long ago that "there's no judge in judgment"—which always reminds me not to put an *e* after the *g*. And I mispronounce to myself the word *relevant* [rel e vant]—stressing the last syllable *vant*, which is not how one says the word in public.

6. Notice the other words that you cannot seem to remember and remind yourself to look them up. For me, it's words with double letters—does *traveler* have two *l*'s? Is it *proceed* or *procede*? Is it *precede* or *preceed*? No matter how often I look up some words, my brain refuses to make the distinction—but by now I know the words to double check.

7. Pay special attention to the special words in your major discipline. One place you don't want to appear less well educated is on final exams and papers in your major field.

8. Everybody tells you this one: Look up words you don't know in dictionaries. It's a good habit. If you take the time to do it, you'll learn new words as well as how to spell them.

9. Read more books. You internalize lots of language, including how words are spelled, just by casual reading. And here, too, mark and look up new words when you can—but not so often that you lose the thread of your text. In the end, spelling is always secondary to meaning, understanding, and pleasure.

10. Play *Scrabble*, do crossword puzzles, learn more word games—anything to make the shape of words more significant to you. (Well, I wanted to round the list off with ten suggestions—this isn't that farfetched, is it?)

Postscript Four

A SHORT GUIDE TO PUNCTUATION

Listed below are general explanations for punctuation. I have included the most common uses for the punctuation marks described. If you know the uses described here, you will be in good shape as a writer. However, be aware that numerous exceptions to all the punctuation rules also exist—exceptions that I have not attempted to cover here. To learn about these, consult the handbook appended to most dictionaries, Strunk and White's *The Elements of Style*, or one of the many writer's handbooks available in libraries, bookstores, or English teachers' offices.

APOSTROPHES [']

1. Indicate that somebody **possesses** or *owns* something. In single nouns or pronouns, place an **'s** at the end of the word: *John's sister*; *the girl's brother*; *the cat's pajamas*.

    For plural words, add the apostrophe, but omit the **s**: *the boys' books*; *the cats' pajamas (meaning more than one boy or cat)*.

    Notable exception: **its**, since the **'s** in this word indicates the abbreviation **it is**.

2. Indicate abbreviation. Use an apostrophe to indicate missing letters: *can't* for *cannot*; *it's* for *it is*.

3. Indicate the plurals of numbers, letters, or words referred to as words: *7's, p's and q's, if's*.

BRACKETS [[ ]]

1. Indicate that the author has added additional or substitute words in a quotation: *"Then she [Susan Smith] voted again,"* or *"Then [Susan Smith] voted again."*
2. Indicate parentheses within parentheses: (*This is parenthetical [this even more so]*).

COLONS [:]

1. Indicate that an example follows: *This is an example of an example following a colon.*
2. Introduce lists of items: *The ark housed the following animals: cats, dogs, chickens, snakes, elephants, and goats.*
3. Introduce quotations in your text. (MLA documentation recommends indenting material five lines or more; when you indent quotes, the indentation substitutes for quotation marks.) Example: *The first paragraph of the Declaration of Independence reads as follows:*
4. Introduce phrases or sentences that explain or illustrate previous ones: *The explanation was clear: the example made it work.*
5. Separate titles from subtitles: *College Writing: A Personal Approach to Academic Writing.*

COMMAS [,]

Note: misplaced or missing commas account for many of our punctuation errors. You may take some comfort in knowing that even experts disagree about some of these so-called rules. Journalists, for example, don't put commas after the next-to-last item in a series; professors most likely do: *The cat, the rabbit*[,] *and the bat.*

In general, commas indicate pauses within sentences. You can usually hear the pause when the sentence is read aloud. I often read aloud to myself to tell me where commas go. However, the following guidelines will remind you more specifically when and where to use commas:

1. Separate two main clauses (complete sentences) joined by **and**, **but**, **or**, **for**, **nor**: *I can run fast, but I can't run far.*
2. Separate words or phrases in a series: *His favorite sports included motorcycle riding, hockey, tennis, golf, fishing, and baseball.*

3. Set off a clause or long phrase that introduces a main clause (the major part of the sentence): *After we attend class, we'll eat lunch and take our afternoon naps.*
4. Set off transitional words from the rest of the sentence: *She asked, however, that she not be quoted. It is not true, for example, that squirrels fly. In other words, writing is easy.*
5. Set off extra, explanatory information not absolutely essential in the sentence: *Toby, a professor of mine, occasionally gives good lectures. That dog, the black one, ate the garbage.* (The same information could be set off in parentheses, which would indicate it was even less essential for an understanding of the sentence.)
6. Set off words that address or exclaim and people who say things:

   "How are you, Paul?" she said.
   "Oh, not so hot," he replied.

7. Introduce or conclude direct quotations: *According to the study by Smith and Rocket, "acid rain is the major cause of the decreasing trout population in Vermont."*

DASHES [—]

1. Mark abrupt changes or breaks in sentences: *It isn't true—or is it?*
2. Set off information not considered essential to the understanding of sentences: *The stock market crash—it was 1929—did my grandfather in.*
3. Summarize earlier items in a sentence: *The amount of unemployment, the price of gold, the availability of oil, the weather—all these influence the amount of taxes we pay.*

   Note: dashes can often be used to set off apparently digressive information in the manner of commas or parentheses; however, they imply that the information is, while slightly off track, essential. Note, too, that the use of dashes to connect loose thoughts (in place of periods or semicolons) is not considered a sign of good writing in the academic world where one's thoughts are not supposed to be loose.

ELLIPSES [. . .   . . . .]

1. Three dots in a quoted passage indicate an omission of one or more words in a quotation: *John argued . . . that he should stay.*

2. Four dots in a quoted passage indicate the omission of one or more sentences, or missing words at the end of a sentence (the fourth dot being the missing period): *Remember Lincoln's opening words "Four score and seven years ago. . . ."*

3. Four dots indicate the writer's thoughts trailing off midstream: *a deliberate strategy to convey. . . .*

EXCLAMATION POINTS [!]

Indicate strong emotional statement, either positive or negative, on the part of the writer: *"Stop, you can't go in there!" Henry, I love you!*

Note: use these marks sparingly in academic writing as they imply overstatement—and academics are wary of overstatement. Also use them sparingly in personal writing as they give away too much emotion and "tell" the reader how to feel.

HYPHENS [-]

1. Divide a word of more than one syllable at the end of a line.

2. Connect some compound concepts: *brother-in-law, know-it-all.*

3. Connect some compound modifiers: *student-centered program, fast-sailing ship, four-cylinder engine.*

4. Connect prefixes to some words (emphasize the prefix): *pre-literate, post-operative, re-write.*

5. Connect compound numbers between 21 and 99: *twenty-one, ninety-nine, one hundred thirty-five.*

6. Indicate that all the numbers between the first and last numbers are included: *1980-85, pp. 34-85.*

   Note: like commas, there is some debate about when and what to hyphenate. Look up particular words in a current dictionary to be absolutely certain. Note too that a writer may hyphenate whenever she wishes to create a special emphasis in a word or phrase.

PARENTHESES [( )]

1. Set off explanatory material the author does not consider necessary to understand the basic meaning of the sentence: *In 1929 (the year the stock market crashed) he proposed to his first wife.* (The same information set off by commas would be considered more essential to the sentence.)

2. Allow an author to use a **double voice** and comment about her subject from a different perspective, often ironic: *Parentheses allow an author to comment on his text from an ironic perspective (whatever that means).*
3. Enclose *(1)* numbers and *(2)* clarifying information about numbers and acronyms in a sentence: *forty-seven (47), NFL (National Football League).*

PERIODS [.]

1. End sentences. Bring readers to a full stop. Period. (Is used the same way with full sentences or deliberate sentence fragments.)
2. Indicate abbreviations in formal (*Dr., Jr.*) and informal (*abrv., esp.*) writing.

QUESTION MARKS [?]

1. Indiate that a question has been asked: *What do you want?*
2. Indicate an author's uncertainty: *(Sp?)*

QUOTATION MARKS [" "]

1. Enclose direct quotations: *"What's for dessert?" she asked.*
2. Enclose words or phrases borrowed from others: *It really was "the best of times," wasn't it?*
3. Enclose titles of poems, stories, articles, songs, chapters, TV programs: *Who wrote the poem, "To an Athlete Dying Young"? Faulkner's "Barn Burning" is ultimately a comic story. My favorite chapter in this book is "Finding Your Voice."*

Note: to indicate a quotation within a quotation, use single marks (' ') instead of double: *"She said 'It really isn't necessary,' but that didn't stop him long."*

SEMICOLONS [;]

1. Can be used in place of a period when you want to imply a close relationship to the following sentence; *here that's what I want to imply.*
2. Replace commas in a series of phrases when the phrases include commas: *Considering the circumstances, it is dangerous to run, when you can walk; talk, when you can listen; and read, when you can write.*

Note: semicolons are most frequently used in quite formal language; they are especially common in prose before the twentieth century; academics are fond of them since they imply formal relationships and make sentences long—and long sentences appear to be more intellectually rigorous; whether they are more rigorous or simply more ponderous is a question for you to decide.

ITALICS [UNDERLINING]

1. Indicate special emphasis in typed and handwritten papers: *He was very careful to underline all the examples, except this one.*
2. Indicate the titles of published works, including books, movies, albums/tapes/CD's, and collections of articles, stories, poems, and essays: *For Whom the Bell Tolls is a novel by Ernest Hemingway. Only a few successful plays; such as The Sound of Music, also become successful movies. My favorite tape is Bruce Live. The story "Burning" can be found in The Portable Faulkner.*
3. Indicate words and letters being referred to as words and letters: *Is the correct word to indicate a struggle founder or flounder? The letter x is the least used word in the alphabet, isn't it?*

Index

A

Abstracts, 105
Academic community, 3–10
American Psychological Association, 170, 174
Analogy, 83–85
Analysis, 91, 94
Analytical essays, 78–89
Apostrophes, 202
Argument, 92
Assignment
essay, 79–80
written, 54–57
Assumptions in research, 144–45
Attitudes toward writing, 11
Audience, 53–61
Autobiography, 73–74
deductive, 73
focus of, 73–74
inductive, 73
scope of, 73

B

Belief, creation of, 6, 68–69
Book reviews, 108
Brackets, 203
Brainstorming, 29–30

C

Card catalogue, 162
Colons, 203
Communication, 12–13
Comparison, 83–85
Composing, 123–32
Computers, 125, 163
backing up files on, 192
desktop publishing with, 190
drafts and, 192–93
editing with, 190
final copies and, 193
formatting thought and language with, 190

generating ideas with, 191
information retrieval/transfer
and, 191
journals and, 192
printing and, 193
revising with, 191, 192
sharing and, 193
spell-checkers and, 190, 193, 200
typing with, 190, 192
word processing programs and, 190, 192
Conceptual mapping, 26–27
Council of Biology Editors, 170, 174–75
Critical reviews, 107

Essays
expository, 78–88
interpretive, 90–99
Evaluation, 95–97
of research paper, 147
of sources, 163–65
journal, 40–41
Evidence, 6–7
Examinations, essay, 98–99
Exclamation points, 205
Experiential writing, 62–74
Experiments, 156
Explanation, 80–81
Exploratory writing, 14–17
Exposition, 65, 78
Expressive writing, 14–17

D

Dashes, 204
Definition, 81–83
Description, 65
Dialogue, 65
Diaries, 44–45
fictional, 116–18
Dillard, Annie, 63–64
Direct quotation, 166–69
Documentation, 7, 166–76
in computer science, 175
mechanics of, 167–69
Draft, 124–25
discovery, 146–47
sharing of, 57–58

E

Editing, 59, 127–31
Education Resources Information Center (ERIC), 163
Elements of Style, The, 202
Ellipses, 204–205
Emotion in narrative, 70

F

Facts, 70
Fiction, 116
Figurative language, 70–71, 84–85
First-person point of view, 65
Five-paragraph themes, 108–109
Format
of essays, 98
of imaginative writing, 115–16
of personal narrative, 71
Formula
book review, 108
topic sentences, 102–103
Freewriting, 24–26
Frost, Robert, 93–94

G

Generalizations, 102
Gillman, Charlotte Perkins, 94
Guides, 161–62

H

Hyphens, 205
Hypothetical situations, 120

I

Imaginative
language, 13–14
writing, 112–22
Imitation, 119
Indices, 162
Informal writing, 14–17
Information sources, 63
Interpretation, 92–95
of fiction, 94
of poetry, 94
Interview
documentation of, 168–69
observation, 155–56
silence in, 153
Introduction, writing of, 126
Italics, 207

J

Jobs, writing about, 66–67
Journal writing, 15, 16, 32–49
how to, 43–49

L

Language
authentic, 70
figurative, 70
level of, 59
use of, 12
Leading questions, 153
Letters, 16–17, 116–17
Library, 161–63
List making, 27–28

Listening, 156
Logs, 44–45
research, 142–49

M

Mapping, conceptual, 26–27
Martin, Steve, 96
Metaphor, 84
Modern Language Association
(MLA), 170
format of documentation,
171–73

N

Name/title system of documentation, 171–73
Name/year system of documentation, 174–75
Narrative writing
action in, 69
detail in, 69–71
emotion in, 70
fictional, 116–18
personal, 65–73
Newspapers, 162–63
Notebooks, 44–45
Novel, 13
Novelists, 63
Number system of documentation, 175

O

Objectivity, 7–8
narrative and, 65
Observation
journal and, 33
research and, 155–56
voice and, 186

Outlines, 28–29
for draft, 124–25

P

Paraphrase, 169
Parentheses, 205
Parody, 120
Periodicals, 162
Periods, 206
Personal narratives, 65–73
Personal writing, 14–17
Persuasion, 6, 92
Physical sciences, 175
Physical world, 5
Plays, 13
Poems, 13–14
Poets, 63
Problems solving, 20–30
freewriting and, 24–26
Proofreading, 58, 60
Publication, 58, 59
Purpose
of essay, 80–86
of writing, 4

Q

Question marks, 206
Questions
answering of, 109–110
asking of, 21–24
interview, 151–54
journalists, 106–107
research, 135–40, 145–46
research log and, 143
Quotation, direct, 166–69
Quotation marks, 206

R

Reading, 37–38
Re-creation, 119–20

Reference
journal as, 39–40
for research paper, 170–75
Relativity, 8
Reports, 105–107
journalistic, 106–107
Research
assumptions in, 144–45
and autobiography,
books and periodicals as,
160–65
people and places as,
151–57
resources and, 145–46
use of authority and, 166–75
Research logs, 142–49
Research paper, 135–36
planning of, 146–47
Research questions, 135–40
Resources, 151–57
books and periodicals as,
160–65
places as, 154–57
people as, 151–54
Reviews, 107
Revision, 125–31
research paper, 148
Rewriting, 125–31
Roethke, Theodore, 94
Role playing, 30, 119

S

Self-awareness, 38–39
Self-exploration, 65–73
Semicolons, 206–207
Set pieces, 101–110
Similes, 84
Slant, 56
Sources; *see also* Resources
evaluation of, 163–65
of information, 63
Speaking, 12
Speculation, 35

Spelling, 199–201
  games and, 201
  reading and, 200
Style manual, 170
Subjectivity, 7
Subtitles, 127
Summary, 104, 169
Synthesis, 91–92

T

Talking, 53–54
Tape recording, 154
Teachers, writing for, 54–57
Teaching, 56
Term paper, 17
Theme
  of autobiography, 73–74
  imaginative writing, and,
    113–14
Thesis statements, 103–104
Thinking, 11–18
Time in personal narrative,
  67–68
Titles, 127
Topic sentences, 102–103
Truth, 6

U

Underlining, 207

V

Visual writing, 26–27
Voice, 97
  arrangement of, 179–80
  content of, 179
  evolution of, 180
  finding of, 177–86
  imaginative writing and,
    114–15
  interpretive essays and,
    97–98
  style of, 178–79

W

Word processor, 125, 189–93
Wordiness, 127–29
Writing group guidelines
  to the audience, 197–98
  to the class, 194–95
  to the writer, 195–96
Written assignment, 54–57